DATE		
MAR 21 '83		
MAY 24 '83		
MAR 7 '84		
APR 25 '85		
MAY 12 '89		
JUL 10 1998		
MAY 22 2002		

The Family Camping Handbook

The Family Camping Handbook

A Complete Guide to Camping in North America
Jerome and Alyson Knap

Pagurian Press Limited

Distributed by
Publishers Marketing Group
A Baker & Taylor Company
Executive Offices
1515 Broadway, New York, N.Y. 10036

Distribution Center
Gladiola Avenue, Momence, Ill. 60954

ISBN 0-88932-016-0 (Paper)
ISBN 0-919364-96-9 (Cloth)
Printed and bound in the United States

For Joanne and Ed

*May their children have the opportunity
of experiencing a wilderness camping trip*

PICTURE CREDITS

Thanks are due to the following organizations for the use of photographs: British Columbia Government (page 141); Frostline Kits (pages 22, 86, and 128); Gerry Division, Outdoor Sports Industries (pages 98, 100, 132, and 133); Gouvernement du Québec (page 112); National Park Service, U.S. Department of the Interior (page 119); Ontario Ministry of Industry and Tourism (pages 55, 102, 155, and 162); Ontario Ministry of Natural Resources (page 179); Stow-A-Way Sports Industries (page 167); Thomas Black and Sons Canada Ltd. (pages 44, 50, 57, and 58).

Contents

Introduction

Fads and fashions spring forth in this world like mushrooms after a warm summer rain. But sometimes a fad becomes a permanent fixture. Why, we don't know. Probably because the underlying appeal comes from deep within man's nature and instincts.

One pastime that began as a fad among wealthy and jaded city people and became a permanent fixture was camping. Sure, men have always camped on this continent—the early voyageurs, the frontiersmen, and the mountain men. And the Indians following the buffalo camped before them. The Old West had its campers too—hunting tribes and pastoral nomads. However, these persons all camped because of necessity. Large settlements and permanent dwelling places were not feasible in their way of life. But to go out and live in the wilderness in a temporary shelter just for the fun of it, just for the experience—that was something new, surely a passing fad.

It has not passed. Northern rivers that have not been paddled by white men since the days of the fur-trading brigades are being paddled today. Trails untrod since the days of the early mountain men are being backpacked today. And campgrounds in many of our parks are so crowded that park authorities have had to instigate a reservations system so that campers are assured of a place to pitch their tents. The time when a camper will not be able to visit the same national park each year is around the corner.

The reasons for the camping boom are not easy to explain. More leisure time, higher incomes, and better highways and transportation systems are some of the reasons. The elements of fad and fashion come into it as well. To go camping, particularly backpacking or canoe tripping, is an "in" thing, particularly for the young. A greater awareness and interest in wild things and wild places are contributing factors. Our growing population is another but, in our opinion, none of these are important enough, strong enough even when combined, to account for this boom.

The main reason for the boom is that now, since we have amassed the trappings of a comfortable and affluent life, we hunger for the quiet and simple things—clean air, small wavelets lapping on a rocky shore, the quiet chirping of birds as the sun sinks behind the western hills. We long for the smell of wood smoke and the deeply satisfying feeling after a long day of paddle, pole, and portage.

We want to get away from "it"—the sophistry and sophistication of our society, but frequently we bring "it" with us in the form of tent slums. Moderation and wisdom are not easy commodities to find among mankind. Throughout this book, we have tried not only to describe the techniques and equipment needed for any family camping trip, but also to impart the essence of camping. Man, like all living things on this earth, is a user. This is what nature intended him to be. But man must use with wisdom and moderation. Alas, he has not always done so. And campers are no exception.

If camping is to have any meaning, it must be a communion between man and nature. Man sprang from nature. He is a part of it, but only a small part, and conversely nature is a part of man.

CHAPTER 1

Camping for All Ages

Until very recently, camping, like all other outdoor pursuits, was a pastime of a small minority. Two decades ago you could hike over the trails of the high Sierras and not encounter another party in a week of walking. Not today. Twenty years ago, 90 percent of the campgrounds along the major thoroughfares, let alone the ones on the back roads, were yet to be built. The campgrounds in the national parks were much smaller, and even in summer, were half empty. No more.

All of us come to the outdoors in our own way and in our own time. There is no best or only way. The backpacker may find the campgrounds of the roadside parks as confining as his house in the city. The canoe tripper may find a backpacking trip too much of a drudgery. Only a pole and paddle and a wild river bring peace to his soul. The automobile camper may find the wilds too forbidding, too unfamiliar, and too rigorous for peace of mind and comfort.

It is estimated that 60 million people on this continent—a quarter of the population—camp or have camped at one time or another. It is one of the most popular family recreations. There are no age barriers, except those created by people themselves. Campgrounds—private, public, and wilderness —have no age restrictions for admittance.

Modern camping equipment has made outdoor living as comfortable as living in any house. In fact, there's less work—no lawn to mow, no vacuuming, and no dusting. Camp meals are lighter and less complex, and certainly no more difficult to cook on a gasoline or propane camp stove than on an electric range at home. Erecting a modern tent is not much more difficult than setting up a folding lounge chair. Even older people with medical problems need not feel apprehensive about camping on a modern campground. Some campgrounds have a doctor on call 24 hours a day.

Modern camping equipment is fairly easy to use. If the demonstration in the store was not adequate, there will be many campers on any campground who will be glad to show you how. In campgrounds on state, provincial, and national parks, the park rangers will be glad to help, and on private campgrounds so will the proprietors.

In fact, in several of the state parks in Ohio, novice campers can rent a

Camping is one of the most popular of family recreations.

campsite and all basic equipment and also get instructions and help in pitching a camp from trained park rangers. The cost of this service is $6 per night with a maximum stay of 7 nights. Reservations have to be made two weeks in advance.

You can make a camping trip as comfortable or as rugged as you wish, as restful or as exhausting as you need. You can have solitude in the wilderness, or bustle and company in a beach-front campsite. You can camp on public land free of charge, or stay in a luxury park with heated swimming pools, tennis courts, and riding stables.

Camping with Kids

To say that no child is too young to camp is not really true. However, a baby can begin his camping life just as soon as he has established his feeding schedule, long before he is a year old. Before we become relegated to the subhuman level of child abusers, let us point out that camping is no different, no

Dogs can be taken camping as well, but they must be kept on a leash or tied. On backpacking trips, they can even carry their own load. But remember that dogs are not allowed on the hiking trails of national parks.

less comfortable, than the home life of fifty or sixty years ago, without running water, electrical conveniences, and central heating.

Children can be taken on almost any kind of camping trip. An infant in diapers can ride in a kiddy carrier on a mother's back while she hikes up a mountain trail. Kids seem to get their sea legs quicker than adults in a canoe. If they have life preservers, they are safe enough, although you wouldn't want to run any white water while children are in the canoe. We have more to say about this in our chapter on canoe tripping.

In some ways, infants and toddlers present less of a problem than older kids who may be out getting into devilment of one sort or another. For this reason, parents and older siblings should ride shotgun a bit more energetically and cast a supervisory eye with greater regularity than at home. A bit of a scouting trip into the hinterland beyond the campsite is a good idea, just to spot any potential hazards or trouble areas that may have to be declared out-of-bounds.

For infants, taking along enough canned baby foods is not a problem,

Campgrounds have no age restrictions for admittance. Toddlers can be taken on almost any kind of camping trip, even backpacking trips on Mother's back.

even on a short backpacking trip. Take only small, one-serving jars so that you don't have to worry about refrigeration.

Dealing with diapers is no problem on a car camping trip. The disposable kind can simply be wrapped up and deposited in garbage cans near the campsite. For the backpacker or canoe tripper, regular cotton diapers are best. One cannot leave the disposable type buried with other human waste because the plastic materials in them are virtually indestructible. And packing out soggy diapers is neither practical nor pleasant. Cloth diapers can be washed as necessity dictates, and left to dry and bleach in the sun. The sun's rays have a sterilizing effect as well. On an automobile camping trip, it is often possible to take along a folding crib or even a playpen. A piece of netting tucked all around will protect the child from mosquitoes and other pests.

Rainy days in camp can be a drag for adults, let alone kids. The only way to cope is to bring along books and games. For young children, a favorite toy or two is a must as well. Many young children feel more secure when going to bed with the familiar face of a fluffy dog or teddy bear sleeping beside them. By and large, children take to camping like young otters to water. For them it's a big adventure. Even more important than that, it's a good way to teach kids the wonders and joys of the out-of-doors. Kids that are turned on by the out-of-doors are not likely to get turned on by pills and dope.

Dogs in Camp

It's a sad fact that dogs are becoming a serious nuisance in our camp-grounds. They are something of a nuisance in our cities as well. Too many of them are nothing but ill-mannered beasts—untrained and unmanageable. It's not the dog's fault, of course, but that's hardly an excuse.

If you want to camp with a dog, that's fine. We do. But you must remember that your beloved family pet may be a yapping pest to someone else. Dogs can also be messy, so you must clean up after them. Take them on walks away from paths, nature trails, and camping sites. In most, if not all campgrounds, dogs must be tied up or kept on a leash. They must also be kept away from beach areas, and they must be kept quiet. Dogs are not allowed on the hiking trails of national parks and some state and provincial parks.

If you are backpacking into national wilderness areas or camping on public land, keep your dog on a leash or tied up, so that he does not disturb or chase wildlife. The exception here would be a dog that is trained to walk at heel without a leash and can be stopped from chasing anything with the world "no." We have found that the dogs of duck hunters and upland game-bird hunters are generally much better trained than family pets. And, by the way, there's no reason why any big dog cannot carry his own load on a backpacking trip. Many an old-time mountain man had leather paniers for his dog. The Gerry Division of Outdoor Sports Industries makes modern nylon saddlebags for dogs.

Chapter 2

Under Canvas

The tent is the most important and probably the most expensive piece of equipment in a camper's inventory. When that tent is pitched, the camper has a home. Indeed, many peoples of the world—the hunting tribes of the American plains, the sheep herders of the Mongolian grasslands, and the desert tribesmen of the Mid-East—have found no more superior shelter for their nomadic mode of life than a well-pitched tent.

When buying a tent, make sure that it fits your needs. Ask yourself the following questions: how will it be transported to your campsite—by automobile, packhorse, boat, canoe, or backpack? Will the tent be used for more sedentary camping, staying in one spot for several days, or will it be used mainly as an overnight shelter on canoe trips or cross-country automobile trips? Will it be used mainly during the spring, summer, and autumn months, or will it be used in the winter as well? Do the areas where you usually camp get lots of rain or lots of wind? Finally, how many campers will be using the tent?

Essentially there are two types of tents. One is the trail or hiker's tent. This type is designed to be light, easy to erect and take down, and to provide basic shelter. The second type is the general or family camping tent. It is usually roomier and more comfortable, hence heavier and bulkier.

Trail tents come in different forms. The oldest and best known is the familiar pup tent. The simplest is just a big plastic "bag" with one end held open by air-inflated struts. Such a two-man tent weighs only about two pounds. The pyramid tent is another trail tent. The quick-to-erect igloo is still another. Then there are a number of ingeniously designed lightweight nylon tents made especially for backpackers and mountaineers. Some are large enough to sleep four men but still weigh only five or six pounds.

One of the best ways to select a tent is to visit a dealer who has a large selection erected for display. Camping shows and sportsmen's shows are also

The cottage tent is the most popular type of family tent. It is relatively easy to erect and is roomy and comfortable.

17

good places to see a large selection of tents. Examine the tents very carefully, and look for features that you want. Do not hesitate to pull down a couple of sleeping bags onto the floor of a trial tent to test for space. Bring a couple of cots into a camping tent.

Tents come in an almost seemingly endless variety of shapes, styles, sizes, colors, and materials, much to the confusion of tyros. Before getting into specifics, let us emphasize that you should always buy the best quality you can afford, and, when in doubt about the size, buy the next size up.

Tents are made of three materials—cotton, nylon or similar synthetic fibers, and plastic. Canvas is, of course, made of cotton fibers, and comes in many grades and in 8, 10, and 12-ounce weights. When treated, it is water resistant. It is fairly heavy and, like all organic material, it rots and mildews. But it is durable. When properly taken care of, a canvas tent will last through many decades of camping.

Nylon is strong and light. It will not rot or mildew. It is completely waterproof, which is fine for shedding rain, but also means that it sweats. That is, water vapor from breathing will condense on the inside, making the tent clammy.

Some of the best tents on the market, particularly the light trail tents for backpackers, are made of blended fabrics using both cotton and synthetic fibers. Plastic is light and waterproof, but it is fragile and tears easily. It is also noisy and highly flammable. Its biggest virtue is its very low price. Plastic tents are so low in price that careless campers do not even bother to take them down, leaving them to litter the countryside.

Most tents of current manufacture have sewn-in floors. The old-time campers would have viewed this with a jaundiced eye. They preferred a floor of fragrant green balsam boughs. So would we, but this rustic luxury is seldom possible today. Our campsites receive too much pressure, too many visitors, to allow the cutting of boughs for floors or beds.

An integral floor can be a dirt-collecting nuisance. If the floor is made of canvas, it can be hard to keep clean. On the other hand, vinyl-coated or rubberized floors are no problem. They can be wiped clean very easily with a damp cloth. However, sewn-in floors are a real boon in bug country. Also, they cut out drafts in cold, wet weather. The width of the floor area is a critical factor in trail tents. An 8-foot length is ample. Such a tent will have room at the head or foot for boots, clothing, cameras, and possibly even a packsack. But you should figure on 36 inches of width for each camper. This is the width of most sleeping bags. Every tent should be equipped with a screened-in doorway and have screens on all of the windows.

Novices may think that trail tents are small so that they will be light. This is not the only reason. In many areas, particularly in the mountains, it is difficult to find a flat area large enough to pitch a big tent. Also, small tents generally require fewer guy ropes and stakes. Some do not require any stakes at all. This again is a boon in rocky areas where the soil is too shallow to hold stakes. Small tents have less wind resistance, which may be important on ocean beaches or on windswept mountain ridges. For very windy areas, low-lying tents are a must. We prefer trail tents that have at least one point high enough for an adult to stand. Such tents are much more comfortable and convenient. The highest point may be in the center or at the entrance.

Tents for general camping come in many different shapes and styles as well. Some manufacturers have over a dozen different models in their selection. The basic quality to look for is roominess. After all, the tent will be up for a few days or even a week or more, and most likely you will be using camp cots to sleep on. You may even have a folding table and chairs with you. Your tent should have enough room for all this and more. Is there enough space in the tent for an entire family on a rainy day? You will find that tents with vertical walls allow better use of all floor space than tents with sloping walls. General camping tents are nearly always made of canvas, so nothing must touch the walls during a rain, or else water will soak right through.

Remember that you will need more space as the kids grow. A tent that is large enough for a pair of adults and a couple of toddlers may not be big enough when the toddlers become older. Investigate the possibility of two small tents rather than one big one. This will give the adults some privacy.

Tents for warm-weather camping should be light in color to reflect the sun. They should have big windows for ventilation. For foul weather or winter camping, choose a tent with an awning or a storm flap over the entrance.

Ventilation is of crucial importance in nylon tents. Every nylon tent should be well ventilated to prevent condensation. Nylon does not breathe. As we said earlier, it is totally waterproof. Good ventilation ensures that the condensed water can escape. Some nylon tents have ventilation vents, others have long, narrow, screened-in windows. Still others have a screened-in strip at the ridge. These strips are covered by a fly sheet. Manufacturers of modern nylon tents have learned how to cope with condensation. Another drawback of nylon tents is their propensity for leaking at the seams. This again is because nylon is totally waterproof. Canvas, when it becomes wet, seals the stitching holes at the seams, but not nylon. The stitching holes have to be sealed with a chemical sealer or covered by a waterproof cloth.

If you intend to backpack with a tent, select one that has a telescopic or sectional frame which can be collapsed to take up a minimum of space. Many of today's tents have outside frames. Such frames are vastly superior to inside frames or poles because they allow better use of inside space. They are also easier to erect.

A flysheet equipped with tie tapes is a handy item on every camping trip. When it is over a tent, it makes the tent cooler in the summer, warmer in winter, and much more waterproof during a rainstorm. The flysheet also can be used as a wind break, a cover for gear and firewood, a lean-to, or a roof over a dining area.

To spot quality in tents, look at the seams. They should be straight and tight. Double stiching is best. Grommets that are stitched in are stronger than those that are simply punched in. Look for extra thickness of fabric at corners and at the peak. These are the places that are subject to strains and stresses. Zippers can be either nylon or metal, but they should be heavy duty. Nylon zippers are preferable.

Waterproofing a Tent

Every new canvas tent is treated by its manufacturer to make it waterproof or water repellent. With better-quality tents, such waterproofing will last up to several seasons, depending on how much actual use the tent gets. But sooner or later, every canvas tent has to be waterproofed. This presents no serious problem for the modern camper. There are a number of waterproofing solutions on the market, most of which are silicone based. They come in both paint-on or spray-on containers. We have used both with excellent results. To apply, simply erect the tent and then spray or brush the solution on.

The spray-on solutions in aerosol cans are more convenient to use, but they are also more expensive. With spray-on cans one has a tendency to use more solution than is needed. Somehow there is an irresistible urge to give the canvas an extra shot, just to be sure. Also, areas can be easily missed if the sprayer is not careful. The paint-on treatment is slower, but cheaper. Backpackers should be aware that waterproofing does have a tendency to make canvas heavier.

The do-it-yourselfer and the purist can make their own waterproofing solution. One way is to melt paraffin wax in turpentine, a pound of wax to a gallon of turpentine. The turpentine should be heated in hot water, not directly on a stove, because of its highly flammable nature. Shave the paraffin wax into the turpentine in small slivers so that it will melt quickly.

The solution can then be painted on the tent. About three gallons are needed to waterproof a 9-foot by 9-foot umbrella tent. Benzine can be substituted for turpentine, but it makes the canvas a little stiffer. The big disadvantage of this solution is that paraffin-treated canvas is highly flammable.

A better homemade solution for fairly tightly woven fabrics is one of alum and lead acetate dissolved in soft water. In one tub, mix one-quarter pound of lead acetate in a gallon of hot soft water. Then dissolve one quarter-pound of alum in a gallon of hot soft water in another tub. After letting the lead acetate solution settle for a few hours, pour all but the dregs on the bottom into the tub with the alum and soft-water solution. Then soak the tent in this mixture for 10 or 12 hours. After rinsing the tent out in clear water, hang it up to dry. The advantage of this waterproofing method is that it is sparkproof. However, it is not as effective in repelling water as the paraffin-based solution, hence it is more suited for tents made of heavier, tightly woven fabric.

Every camper should carry with him a candle or two, a small block of paraffin or, even better, beeswax for emergency waterproofing of small areas. Just rubbing some paraffin wax or beeswax over the leaky area will waterproof it temporarily.

Tent Pegs

Usually stakes or tent pegs come with the tent. More often than not, these are made of aluminum and nestle into one another for compactness. But such tent pegs are not always the best choice. Aluminum tent pegs have the virtue of being light, but they also tend to be frail and bend out of shape far more easily than they should.

Steel stakes are a good bet for all-around use when weight is no serious handicap. They are excellent for automobile camping. Pegs of high impact plastic are also quite good. They are relatively inexpensive and surprisingly durable. And since they frequently come in bright colors, they are easy to spot and seldom get left behind, even when camp is broken in twilight. Wooden stakes are rarely used today. They split far too easily. They just do not have the durability of steel or even tough plastic.

Most stakes are designed to be driven into the ground with a mallet or the blunt end of an axe or hatchet. This means that they need fairly soft, rock-free earth. For pebbly ground, the skewer or screw-type stakes are hard to beat. They are screwed into the ground, not pounded. Such pegs can also be used on soft forest loam. Another excellent peg is the V-shaped stake of spring wire. They can be easily pushed into the ground but are hard to pull straight up because they make the law of leverage work for them. They are suitable for all-around use and ideal for camping on rocky areas where the soil is very shallow. They do not need much soil to grab hold. Another good feature is their relatively low cost.

Family Tents

The *wall tent* is an old camping standby. It is a classic. It is spacious and has ample head room. It serves as the summer home of Eskimos and Indians in Canada's far north, and every summer it houses thousands of forest-fire fighters across the entire continent. Indeed, it is the service tent of the U.S. Forest Service. It is the work horse of outfitters who cater to campers and big-game hunters and, in Africa, it is the most popular safari tent.

The wall tent's main virtue is its spaciousness and amount of head room. When pitched on a floor of boards, it becomes a very comfortable shelter. A stovepipe can easily be shoved through the roof, and a small wood burning stove will heat the tent even in freezing weather.

The *umbrella tent* has become popular among automobile campers. It is a good tent. It has plenty of head room and the walls are vertical enough so that little internal space is lost. Choose one that has a window across from

Tents today come in a seemingly endless variety of shapes, styles, sizes, colors, and materials. Use mainly determines what type to buy.

the door for cross ventilation. Most modern umbrella tents have no inside poles. The poles are on the outside of the corners. Although this gives more room inside or, at least more usable room, it makes the tent heavier. Also the tent with outside poles is not as easy or quick to erect. With the older umbrella tents, all the camper had to do was pound in the four corner stakes and then telescope the center pole and the tent was up.

The *schooner tent* is another relatively new design. It also gets its name from its shape, that of the prairie schooner or covered wagon of the early western pioneers. For its relatively large size, the schooner tent is very quick to erect. The tent is held up by three-piece fiberglass ribs. On calm days no pegs are needed to keep it up. Another fine feature of the schooner is that for a big tent, it folds into a fairly compact bundle. We have used a schooner tent on many camping trips and have been very satisfied with it.

Undoubtedly the *cottage tent* is today's most popular family camping

This tent is a modern version of the pup tent. It is a light and very useful trail tent.

tent. Like the explorer or mountaineer tent, the cottage tent comes in a variety of designs, models, and sizes. Some cottage tents are as large as small summer cottages. A variety of options such as screened-in porches, separate bedrooms, and room dividers can be attached to some of the models.

The cottage tent nearly always has vertical walls which allow for maximum use of all inside space. The poles and frame that hold it up are all on the outside. The cottage tent is the ideal tent for large families.

Trail Tents

The *pup tent* is one of the oldest and simplest tents made. It is extremely popular among Boy Scouts as an overnight camper. The pup tent is the original trail tent. It is just a sleeping tent, offering little room for anything but sleeping. Its biggest virtue is its low cost. It is also easy to pitch. It can be useful as a second tent or as a bedroom for a couple of kids on a family camping trip. A two-man pup tent, 5-½ x 7 feet, is probably the most popular size, but it really is a little too small for two men.

As the name suggests, the *pyramid tent* is shaped like a pyramid. It can be supported by a center pole or suspended from a stout branch of a big tree or from an external tripod of saplings. It is one of the best tents for shedding rain or snow. It is also one of the oldest designs still on the market, and was very popular among prospectors and timber cruisers. The pyramid tent, 7 x 7 feet, has ample room for two men, while a 9 x 9-foot tent is big enough for three.

The *Baker tent* is a sort of wall tent with the front wall raised to form an awning. The front is therefore open. The Baker is a poor tent for country where bugs are troublesome, unless a screen of mosquito netting is hung across the open wall.

Contrary to popular opinion, the Baker tent was not designed for warm-weather camping because of its open front. The Baker is actually a very good cold-weather tent. A fire backed by a reflector wall will keep a 6 x 8-foot Baker tent warm even in late fall. The secret is to build the fire below the awning so that the heat is trapped. The awning of the Baker tent, and indeed perhaps the entire tent, should be treated with spark-resistant chemicals. The fire should be kept small. Do not burn pine or spruce—they throw too many sparks. A 6 x 8-foot Baker tent is light enough for backpacking or canoe tripping and will easily accommodate two men plus their gear.

The *igloo tent*, as the name suggests, is in the shape of an Eskimo igloo. It is one of the newer designs. One of its virtues is that it is easy to erect and needs no tent pegs. One model comes with outside rods of fiberglass, while another has inflatable struts. The model with fiberglass rods erects much like an umbrella. It is one of our favorites.

The igloo tent is not the ideal tent for backpacking into the mountains, or to take on a canoe trip where long portages have to be made. It is a little too heavy and bulky for that. But the 7-foot igloo tent is fine for canoeing where the portages are short, and it will sleep two men comfortably. The 9-foot igloo tent is best for automobile camping or for a horseback trip with pack ponies.

The *cartop tent* is a European development. Basically, it is a small tent perched on top of an automobile roof. When taken down, it looks much like a cartop carrier. One virtue is that it is easy and quick to erect. Another is that it is carried on the roof of the car, a place that is seldom used to carry any load. This is no small feature when you consider that the cartop tent is mainly used on European compact cars.

The main disadvantage of the cartop is that all of the models we have seen appear fragile. Most do not have much room, and the fact that you have to get into them by climbing a ladder would not appeal to many people. Since the cartop tent can be erected only on a cartop, its use is limited to automobile camping.

24

The igloo tent is one of the newer designs. It is easy to erect and needs no pegs to hold it down.

The *backpacking tent* is another new development. Nearly all of these tents are made of nylon or dacron or a blend of cotton and synthetic fiber to make them light and durable. Ripstop nylon is probably the most popular material.

There are a large number of different models and styles of explorer tents on the market, each with a distinct trade name. Tney have all been designed with light weight, as well as ease of erectability in mind. Some, of course, are lighter and easier to pitch than others. We prefer tents that have standing room, at least in one portion of the tent.

Backpacking tents can be divided into two major groups—the forest tents designed primarily for camping along forest trails, canoe streams, and wilderness lakeshores, and the alpine tents designed for mountain camping where high winds and even blizzards are common. The true alpine tent has a tunnel entrance, an exhaust vent, a cook hole, a frost liner, and a snow frock valance or snow flaps on all sides.

CHAPTER 3

The RV Revolution—But Is It Camping?

Recreational vehicles designed for outdoor living can be divided into these categories: motor homes, camping vans or mini-motor homes, pickup campers, travel trailers, and fold-out trailers or tent trailers. But can living in these recreational vehicles, except perhaps the tent trailers, really be called camping? We seriously doubt it. Outdoor living? Yes. But camping? No.

A vacation in one of the hard-wall recreational vehicles is much like a vacation in a well-equipped summer cottage or housekeeping cabin. Staying in a home, even a portable home, that may have heating, air conditioning, electric or propane appliances, electric lights, hot and cold running water, toilet, showers, and frequently even wall-to-wall capeting, a full-length mirror, and a television set can hardly be called camping. One cannot even call it "roughing it smoothly."

In our minds, such vehicles completely eradicate the true meaning of camping—the fun of sleeping under canvas. The hard walls shut out the sound of crickets, the songs of evening birds, and even the very smell of the forest.

We are not against motor homes or trailers. They do have their place in outdoor recreation. We know many campers who use these vehicles as base camps at the end of the road. From there, they travel deeper into the wilderness with their tents.

The best way to shop for a recreational vehicle is to rent one first. A two-week vacation in a rec vehicle will give you a good picture of the pitfalls and disadvantages as well as the advantages of owning one. It will show you what features to look for and which are a waste of money. It will give you an idea as to how big a motor home or tent trailer you will need for a comfortable vacation with your family. Indeed, it will show you if the capital investment involved is worth the pleasure. For example, we know of a man who calculated that by investing the $14,000 he intended to spend on a motor home into the

Living in a tent trailer can still be called camping. The tent trailer, after all, is still a canvas shelter, and lets in all the sounds and smells of the outdoors.

mortgage market at the current rates of interest, he could rent a similar motor home for his annual vacation and still have money left over from his interest. He thus avoided all of the problems involved with maintenance and insurance and retained all of his original capital. As he put it, it was like eating his cake and having it too.

By renting first, you have a better chance of avoiding costly mistakes when you buy. However, before laying out your cold hard cash for a rental payment, you should decide what you want including, of course, the advantages and the disadvantages of the different types of rigs.

Motor homes come in many lengths and in varying degrees of luxury. Some of the large ones have bathtubs and as much closet and cupboard space as the average home. Some can even sleep 10 people. One of the big disadvantages of this type is that it is designed basically for travel on good roads, preferably paved highways. Such a motor home is not made to travel on rough logging roads deep into the bush.

Another disadvantage of this type of motor home is the cost—$12,000 and up. This means high rental costs, and there are many places on this continent where one can buy a fine summer cottage on a lake for a lower price than a luxury motor home. Such a cottage will even increase in value. It is, after all, a real estate investment, while a motor home depreciates in value from the day you buy it. Still another disadvantage of the large motor home is its poor gasoline mileage. The gasoline shortages may be over now, but the high cost of gasoline is not, and probably never will be again.

The mini-motor homes are much less expensive to rent and to buy. Their main disadvantage is that they are suitable only for a maximum of two adults and a couple of kids. Since the mini is basically a van, it can handle rougher roads than the bigger motor homes. Its shorter wheel base is better for forest and mountain roads with sharp bends.

The main disadvantage of both of these units is that you cannot park them and then detach a powered vehicle as you can with a trailer. If you want to drive somewhere, you must take the whole rig with you. Some owners of big motor homes tow a compact car behind so that they have some alternate means of transportation once they reach their destination.

Pickup campers vary from single fiberglass shells to large, elaborate, over-the-cab campers with shower and toilet facilities. Mini-campers for the Japanese compact pickups are also available. And, for the do-it-yourselfer, plans are occasionally available for homemade pickup campers in the mechanical hobby magazines such as *Popular Mechanics*, *Popular Science*, and *Mechanics Illustrated*.

If you do not own a pickup, then renting a pickup camper and a pickup truck offer no cost advantages over renting a motor home. Pickup campers are most popular among people who already own a pickup for their farm or business. Some of the newer pickup campers can be detached from the truck bed very readily. Thus it is possible to leave them at a campsite and use the pickup for local transportation. The pickup is certainly a better vehicle for bush roads or logging roads. It will take you where a motor home or even a car could never go. And, of course, a four-wheel-drive pickup is better for back-into-the-bush trips than a standard rear-wheel drive truck.

One disadvantage of a pickup is that it is basically a two or three-man vehicle, unless you are going to have people driving in the back. Also, most pickup campers are not meant for more than four people. In fact, four adults may be too many for comfort. Driving with a big load over the cab in strong winds is no fun, and the gas mileage one gets from a pickup loaded with a big, heavy camper is not good. It can be as low as eight miles per gallon. The great advantage of these rigs is that they are more pleasant to drive than a car towing a travel trailer.

Travel trailers, like motor homes, also come in many lengths, shapes, and degrees of luxury. We are talking here, of course, about recreational trailers, not big mobile homes which require a transport truck cab to move them. Comparing a travel trailer and a motor home of comparable quality, of comparable body construction, of the same length, and of equally luxurious outfitting, the travel trailer is less expensive. It does not, after all, have a motor and a power train. For this reason, many people consider travel trailers a better buy. The main advantage of a trailer is that you can leave it parked at your campsite while you go out sightseeing or shopping with the

Tent trailers come in a variety of sizes. Some are even designed to be towed by the sub-compact cars.

One important feature of a tent trailer is the ease and speed with which it can be erected.

car. The big disadvantage is that driving with a travel trailer behind your car is not easy. Strong winds make towing a travel trailer unpleasant. You cannot drive as fast, and the trailer cuts down on gas mileage.

Before you rent or buy a trailer, make sure that your automobile is powerful enough to pull the extra weight comfortably. This is particularly important if you are traveling in the western mountain states and provinces or in the hot country of the southwest. Heavy-duty shock absorbers and even heavy-duty springs are a must with the bigger travel trailers. Your car will also need a towing hookup and electrical connections. Do not forget to include the installation of these in your budget. If you are a do-it-yourselfer, investigate the trailer hitches that you can install yourself. Some simply bolt onto the frame of your automobile. In all cases, make certain that the size of the ball matches the coupler on your trailer.

Rental agencies for vacation rigs are found in all major towns and cities. The yellow pages of the telephone book will list them under the following titles: motor homes, renting and leasing; mobile homes, renting and leasing; camper renting or leasing; camping equipment, rental. Camping trailers can be found under camping trailers, renting or leasing; or under trailers, renting and leasing. Some of the automobile renting agencies also rent recreational vehicles, particularly motor homes, pickup campers, and even tent trailers. You can actually fly to a location and then rent a motor home there for your vacation, much like renting an automobile.

The cost of renting depends primarily on how luxurious a recreational vehicle you want, and on its size. Small travel trailers can be rented for as low as $100 a week and no mileage charge, while luxury motor homes go up to $450 a week and 10 cents per mile. Pickup campers and mini-motor homes generally run about $125 to $175 a week, plus 5 or 6 cents per mile. Gas and oil are not, of course, included in these rental charges. Tent trailers are the cheapest to rent. They start as low as $50 per week, but $75 per week is about average. Generally there is no mileage rate for tent trailers.

Investigate rental costs carefully. Some agents have no mileage charge for the first 1000 miles They have a higher weekly charge, but it still may work out cheaper than paying mileage if you are not going all that far. Some firms have lower rates in winter—the low season from mid-fall to mid-spring. Also, investigate the possibility of renting recreational vehicles from private individuals. Such rates are generally considerably cheaper. Look in the classified ad sections of the larger newspapers for people with rec vehicles to rent.

Before heading out on your trip with a rented rig, be sure to find out how everything works—the propane stove and refrigerator, the lights, and so on. How do you hook up the electricity? How are the water tanks filled and the waste tanks emptied? Where are the jack, the spare tire, and the tools? If it is a tent trailer, how is it erected and folded?

If you plan on crossing an international border (either U.S.-Mexico or Canada-U.S.), make sure that the rental agreement states that you may take the vehicle across. If it is a privately rented vehicle, get a notarized statement from the owner. You will also need special insurance for crossing the border.

One last tip about renting a rec vehicle. If you intend to rent, reserve early so that you are certain of getting the vehicle you want when you want it. Some rental agents have told us that they are booked six months ahead for the summer vacation season.

Tent Trailers

Outdoor living in a tent trailer can still be called camping. After all, the tent trailer is still a canvas shelter. But the tent trailer is losing the "tent" part of its name. More and more tent trailers are being equipped with hard roofs and even aluminum or plastic walls. Built-in kitchen facilities, such as propane refrigerators and stoves, are also increasingly common, as are electric light hookups and other conveniences.

Aside from preserving at least some of the spirit of real camping, the tent trailer does have some advantages over the travel trailer. For one, it is much less expensive. Prices range from around $600 to $2000. There is also less upkeep. Since the tent trailer weighs less and folds down when it has to be trailered, it is easier to pull. The reduced wind drag and lesser weight make for better gas mileage. Tent trailers, at least the smaller ones, can even be pulled by compact cars. Tent trailers come in a variety of sizes. Some of the larger ones will accommodate up to 8 people in beds that fold out on the ends and sides. A tent trailer that measures only 13 feet overall when folded up for towing will spring out into 23 feet when fully erected. Of course, tent trailers are not as comfortable as travel trailers. They are generally not as luxuriously equipped, nor do they offer the same degree of protection from cold and wet. But canvas walls do let in the sounds of crickets, frogs, night birds, and gentle wavelets lapping softly against a rocky lakeshore, and that is what camping's all about.

Among the features to look for when buying a tent trailer are quality construction and a body or box of aluminum. Aluminum is light and durable and will not rust. Bodies of fiberglass or thermoplastic are, in our opinion, not as good. The steel frame with cross members is best, particularly for off-pavement towing. All steel parts should be painted with rust-resistant paint. Probably the best suspension system is the leaf spring because of its good towing and tracking characteristics. Stabilizer jacks that flip down so that the trailer can be leveled on almost any terrain are another good feature. Few campgrounds are absolutely level. The marks of quality for the canvas part of the camping trailer are the same as those for a good quality tent. The canvas should be stainproof and easy to clean. Fire-resistant canvas is best.

Tire sizes on tent trailers vary. Generally, larger tires provide better road clearance and also last longer. The spare tire should be mounted in a place where it is easily accessible. The size of the tent trailer and the number of people it will accommodate is another important criterion. We have found, from personal experience, that a tent trailer meant for six people is generally too small to accommodate six, especially if they are all adults. A trailer for four usually means two adults and two children. Also, a tent trailer that sleeps eight may not have enough room to seat eight people at meal times. This means eating in shifts unless you can erect a folding table outside or unless your campsite has a picnic table. Keep this in mind when deciding on which tent trailer you want. This is why renting first is a good idea. Once you are actually camping, you will find out whether the tent trailer you have chosen is really big enough to accommodate your family comfortably.

The weights of tent trailers are always given in net weights—without dishes, food, clothing, and other camping gear. Be certain your car will pull a loaded trailer comfortably. We feel that any trailer over 1000 pounds should be equipped with electric brakes. Remember also that mini-trailers do not have much space for extra cargo.

Other features determining the final choice are: propane stoves, refrigerators, heaters, cabinet and storage space, and carpeting. Think of these as luxury features. For example, we feel that a stove inside a tent trailer is not as versatile as a portable stove. The portable stove can be taken on tent trips, while a built-in stove cannot. Also, a built-in stove means that the cooking must be done inside the tent trailer, which not only heats up the interior unpleasantly in warm weather, but somehow is just not a part of camping. It's too much like cooking at home. In case of inclement weather, you can always bring a portable stove inside or rig up a tarp as a lean-to over an outside cooking area. We feel the same way about iceboxes, refrigerators, and heaters.

However, on some trailers the stoves and refrigerators can be swung or slid out. This is an excellent feature. In some cases these kitchen appliances are even accessible when the trailer is folded for traveling. This is a handy feature if you stop for lunch by the roadside. A storage locker that is accessible from the outside is also very handy. Only you can make the final decision because only you know your needs, wants, and how much money you want or can afford to spend.

Many tent trailers offer a wide range of optional features, such as canopies which erect into patios. Some even have completely screened-in patios that can be erected once the tent trailer is up. Extra rooms that can be added on are another feature, as are dividing curtains to give sleeping privacy. Racks for light car-top boats, bicycles, trail bikes, or luggage can be installed on some of the tent trailers with metal roofs.

A floor that is easy to keep clean is a must. This is where carpeting falls down. True, it can be vacuumed, but that means lugging a vacuum cleaner along and staying on campgrounds with electricity. A vinyl floor that can be swept and washed is, in our opinion, a far better bet. Inexpensive scatter rugs can be placed by the bedside so that you don't have to stand on a cold floor with bare feet.

The ease and speed with which the trailer erects is an important feature. The system used to erect the trailer is not too important, as long as it is dependable. On some trailers the tent erects by cranking, while on others hinged pulls elevate the tent. The wing beds on the ends and sides either flip out or pull out. Be sure they do so in a smooth and easy manner. Be sure also that the support bars that hold up the bed are sturdy. Ideally, they should be self storing and should attach to the trailer in the same manner. Why? If they do not, one of them invariably gets lost. We know this from experience. Screened windows on all four sides of a tent trailer are a good idea. In some campgrounds you can only position your trailer in one way. Four cross windows ensure that you will catch breezes from any direction. This is only a small feature, but on a hot sticky summer night it can be an important one. Remember our admonition about light colors on tents for repelling sunlight and therefore being cooler. The same applies to tent trailers.

One last tip. Be sure that it is backed by a comprehensive warranty. All of the major tent trailer manufacturers have them on their products, but not all of the smaller manufacturers do. Buy only from a reputable dealer with a good service department. It is easy to check out a dealer's reputation with the Better Business Bureau or the Chamber of Commerce. All complaints will be on record.

CHAPTER 4

Beds and Bedding—It's All in the Bag

Snow swirled around our tent in huge white clouds. Wind pummeled the fabric mercilessly. With each fresh gust, we snuggled deeper and deeper into our sleeping bags. Thanks to a bit of foresight or perhaps premonition, we had brought with us down sleeping bags. The wind had woken us up several times during the night, but never the cold.

By morning the storm was over. It had dumped twelve inches of snow over the landscape. The abnormally cold temperatures persisted for three days, but this did not cause us undue hardships. We had plenty to eat and warm comfortable beds—the two prime requisites for physical well-being and a sound frame of mind.

To us, the storm was an inconvenience, nothing more. In a way it even brought its own blessing. The cold weather forced the trout to fast for three days, but when the warm weather came again, they went on a real feeding binge. We enjoyed some very fine fishing indeed. And as the alpine flowers bloomed through the melting snow, we got some unusual photographs.

We were much more fortunate than some of the other campers in the mountains. Upon returning, we heard many tales of woe and even worse.

The moral here is that an outdoorsman needs a warm and comfortable bed and a full belly for a successful camping trip. A string of sleepless nights can quickly take the bloom off any camping adventure. It can even ruin it. A person who misses out on a good night's rest for too many nights running cannot function properly for long. And he certainly cannot fully enjoy a day's activities outdoors, regardless of how much he has been looking forward to the occasion.

Sleeping bags have become the universal bedding for campers. The old blanket roll is seldom seen in the woods these days, but where weight and bulk are no major problem, good woolen blankets are still a fine choice for the occasional camper who does not want to invest in a good sleeping bag.

Choosing a sleeping bag depends largely on what type of camping you do and on how much you can afford to spend. There are many designs and styles to choose from, as well as materials, covering fabrics, and construction methods.

What Kind of Insulation?

Pound for pound, waterfowl down is the best insulating material known. Yet not all down is equally good. The best down comes from eiders, a species of northern sea ducks. In the old days, eiders were generally shot to obtain the soft warm down from their breasts. Today the down is picked from the nest. The female eider plucks her own breast down in order to insulate her nest. There are men in northern Canada and in Iceland who partly earn their living by gathering eider down. The picking of down is strictly controlled, and can be carried out only under license. This is to insure that each nest is picked over only once. Down then becomes a renewable resource, with a harvestable crop every year.

Down from other waterfowl species, either ducks or geese, raised in northern climates comes next on the quality list. The down of geese is actually superior to that of ducks, but both are good.

The waterfowl farms of Canada, the northern United States, Scandinavia, and Poland are the chief producers of down. The duck farms of Asia raise many ducks, but their down is not of high quality. The warm climate inhibits heavy down growth.

After down come the various synthetics. The best and warmest of these is Dacron Fiberfill II. The primary advantage of synthetics is that they will not rot or mildew, and of course, they are cheaper. They can also be dry-cleaned fairly readily. However, as far as insulating value goes, they are not nearly as good.

Kapok, a natural fiber made of the seed pods of trees from Indonesia, ranks a poor third as an insulating material. It is inferior to good wool. The main reason for its use as insulation in sleeping bags is its low price. Today, kapok is used only in the cheapest of bags.

Sleeping bags with synthetic insulation are a perfectly good choice for summer camping. Because they are twice as heavy and twice as bulky as down of the same warmth, they are not a good choice for the backpacker or the canoe tripper. They are best suited for automobile camping.

Anyone who intends to do some serious camping, particularly during bad weather, should make the move to down. Down is the only material for the mountain camper, not only because the usual way of getting into the mountains is by shank's mare, but also because nights in the mountains can be chilly, even in mid-summer, and freak snowstorms and cold weather can hit even in early summer. Hikers, backpackers, and canoe trippers will find down sleeping bags the best bet because of their light weight.

In recent years, down-insulated sleeping bags and garments have skyrocketed in price. This is largely due to the high demand for down because of the boom in backpacking, canoe tripping, and mountain camping, while production has not increased. As this trend continues, and there is every indication that it will, down bags will price themselves out of a good portion of the market.

A down sleeping bag can be thought of as a 15-year investment. In fact, with proper care, down bags can be made to last even longer. We have had ours for 10 years, and the bags are probably good for 10 more. A down sleeping bag with a comfort range down to -30° F can be purchased for about $150.

Which Is Your Bag?

Sleeping bags come in three basic styles—rectangular, mummy, and barrel. Rectangular bags are the most popular. They are the roomiest. They come in a variety of sizes, from 6-feet-8-inches long and 50-inches wide to the usual 6-feet-2-inches long and 34-inches wide, plus smaller ones for kids. Because of their relatively large size, they are fairly bulky. For this reason they are best for automobile camping or for tent trailers. They are ideal for people who toss and turn and need lots of room.

Rectangular bags also come in mated pairs, where two bags can be joined to form one double one. They can also be unzipped or unsnapped all around to form a comforter. A down-filled rectangular bag makes a wonderful comforter for a double bed. We know a couple who use one of theirs in their summer cottage inside an attractive cotton cover. When they go camping, they simply take the bag out of the cover. This is an excellent way of getting maximum use out of an expensive sleeping bag.

One disadvantage of rectangular sleeping bags is that they have no hoods for cold-weather camping. Most rectangular bags are insulated with synthetic materials. However, down-insulated ones do exist.

Barrel-shaped bags resemble barrels in a vague sort of way. They bulge out in the middle, with the bottom constricting to almost mummy-size and the top running somewhat narrower. Barrel bags are designed to be more comfortable than the mummy type, yet are smaller and more compact than rectangular bags.

Barrel bags are comfortable for those who sleep mostly on their backs or in the fetal position. However, they do not have the versatility of rectangular bags, and they do not come with hoods for cold-weather camping. For really cold weather, a hood is a must. As high as 20 per cent of your body heat can be lost through an unprotected head.

Mummy-type bags were designed for maximum warmth and compact size. In the old days, mummy-type bags had a reputation of being too confining. This is no longer true. Today's mummy bags are cut more generously and generally have more foot room. They are the best choice for backpackers and canoe trippers because of their light weight and compact size. They are also the warmest bags on the market. Nearly all of them come with hoods that can be drawn over the head and shoulders.

One sign of a good quality bag is found right in the shell. The best bags have outer shells made of synthetic and cotton blends, or entirely of nylon. The inner shell on better bags is generally made of nylon taffeta to avoid that clammy feeling. If your vote goes for down-filled bags, be sure that the shell is made of rip-stop material which will not allow holes or punctures to expand, thus losing down. Also, be certain that the material is tightly woven to insure that your down bag will not shed through the pores of the outer and lining materials.

Colors of sleeping bags are a matter of individual preference. Outer shells come in a variety of colors from blaze orange to forest green. The colors of the inner shells are generally more subdued. Colors that do not show dirt too readily are the most practical.

The construction of sleeping bags varies in the method of baffling. Baffles are simply tubes that connect the insulating material. The best types are box-shaped, slanted box, overlapping tubes, or laminated tubes. The first three of these are the most popular. Overlapping tube construction is generally used in bags designated for sub-zero temperatures. Our advice is simply not to be baffled by the baffles. Forget about the theoretical advantages and disadvantages of one type of baffle over another. Reputable manufacturers of sleeping bags do not make poorly constructed bags.

Another consideration in sleeping bag construction is the inner cut. The inner cut can be described as a cross-sectional view of the sleeping bag if it were cut completely through the middle. There are two types of inner cuts —space-filler or warbled, and differential. In a differential cut, the inner shell is smaller than the outer shell. This gives the bag uniform thickness all around its diameter. The space-filler or warbled cut has an inner shell that is warbled with grooves and ridges. This means that if the inner shell were ripped out, it would be the same width as the outer shell. A sleeping bag of the space-filler cut is narrow in the grooves and wider in the ridges.

Bags with the differential cut are more common because they are somewhat easier to make. However, bags with the warbled cut are probably better for cold-weather camping, at least theoretically. The grooves of the cut insure that there are some air spaces between the inner shell and your body.

Another consideration in sleeping-bag construction is the loft. Loft in sleeping bags simply means the thickness of the bag when fully fluffed out. The thicker the loft, the more insulating power the bag has. Bags meant for sub-zero temperatures—20 or 30 degrees below zero—generally have 10 to 12-inch lofts stuffed with 45 to 55 ounces of down. A down bag meant for summer camping would need only a 4-inch loft and 22 ounces of down.

Do not be too concerned about the thickness of the loft. Again, a reputable maker of sleeping bags will not lie about the bag's cold temperature range. The time to be concerned is when a salesman in a discount house tries to sell you a down sleeping bag of an unknown brand with a 5-inch loft, at the same time claiming that the bag was meant for below zero camping. The bag may be good for below zero temperatures, but only if you are sleeping in a heated cabin.

Another consideration in choosing a sleeping bag is the zipper. Nylon zippers are best. They are more dependable than metal. Coil nylon zippers, now used by some manufacturers, are best of all. Some rectangular sleeping

bags still come with snaps. These are usually more dependable than zippers. Many people are concerned with the openings between snaps, believing that they will let in the cold. This is not the case. Sleeping bags with snaps always have a flap or baffle that comes over to cover the slits. The better bags with zippers also have such a baffle along the entire length of the bag.

The zipper should come all the way down to your feet so that the bag can be fully opened in hot weather. This also allows the bag to be aired without turning it inside out. Many mummy bags have zippers that are too short. We also feel that zippers should open and close from both ends, thus allowing better air circulation in warm weather.

A Word About Liners

Bags today seldom come with cotton liners. But there is a trend towards the use of liners. What is a liner? Simply a bag of cotton, flannelette, or some other easy-to-launder material which acts as a bed sheet in the bag. At one time, all the better bags came with liners and tie strings to tie the liner inside the bag. The tie strings were a nuisance, always tangling.

A liner inside a sleeping bag protects the bag from perspiration and body oils. This may not be too important with a synthetically insulated bag because it can be easily dry-cleaned, but it is important with down bags. Down bags cannot be dry-cleaned. They can, of course, be washed, but the less this is done the better.

Snaps are a better method of keeping liners in a sleeping bag than tie strings. The best way to attach liners to a bag is with Velcro pressure-adhering fasteners—strips with stick-on teeth—the material that Eddie Bauer Co. uses in its line of sleeping bags. Liners can, of course, simply be put into sleeping bags loose. Aside from keeping bags cleaner longer, liners also make sleeping bags warmer if they are made of flannelette or similar material.

The camper who intends to take to the outdoors only during spring, summer, and early fall will find that he needs only one sleeping bag—as long as it can be unzipped from both ends in warm weather. The bag should have a comfort range somewhere between 20 to 65 degrees. The camper who also intends to go on winter camping trips will probably need two bags. The winter bag should have a comfort range to sub-zero temperatures. The temperature rating should depend on the possible lows that can occur in the area where he will camp. For winter camping in the western mountains or in northern Canada, the bag should be rated to 40 degrees below zero. A bag for winter camping in New England, on the other hand, probably need not be rated for more than 20 below zero.

Sleeping bags come in basically three different designs—the rectangular, the barrel, and the mummy. They come with three different types of insulation—down, fiberfill, and kapok. The type of bag and the type of insulation chosen depend on the type of camping, the expected weather, and your pocketbook.

There are also bags on the market that can be described as double bags. They consist of an inner and outer bag, both of which can be used separately in warm weather or together as one bag in cold weather. There are also special mummy inner bags on the market that can make any bag 25 percent warmer. The problem with double bags is that they tend to be bulkier and heavier than one-piece bags of the same comfort range. This may not be a handicap for the snowmobiler who intends to camp out, but it would be for the snowshoer or the cross-country skier who wants to travel ultra light.

Inner mummy bags are generally light and fairly compact. Eddie Bauer's inner mummy bag of goose down weighs a mere 16 ounces.

Bags for Kids

The first thing to consider is: do the kids really need sleeping bags? No doubt they would prefer them. They will tell you that real camping is sleeping in a sleeping bag. However, for automobile camping in the summer months, they will be warm enough under good wool blankets. Also the less expensive bags with synthetic insulation are suitable for summer automobile camping. The extra bulk and weight are not important. However, do not over-economize on kids' sleeping bags. Some people seem to think that any cheap bag is fine. After all, the kids will only wreck it or outgrow it. But there are cheap bags on the market that will not keep a child warm on a cool summer night.

There are, however, legitimate reasons why sleeping bags for children should be cheaper than bags for adults. There is no question that kids will quickly outgrow the smaller bags. This may be reason enough to cancel any thought of investing in a down bag. With small children, bedwetting may also be a problem. This may again rule out a down bag, since bags with synthetic insulation can be dry-cleaned.

There are no really perfect solutions. Kids old enough to go on canoe trips and backpacking trips are probably big enough for an adult-sized bag, even if you have to tie it off two thirds of the way down so that the child won't sleep too deeply in the bag. In the case of down bags, this wouldn't matter. Down bags breathe despite their nylon shells, so a child cannot suffocate in one.

For smaller children, there are several possible solutions. Some manufacturers, such as Alpine Design, make down bags for kids. Or, the so-called foot sacks may fit the bill. These are special sleeping bags designed for the lower half of the body. They generally come equipped with a drawstring at the waist. Foot bags are for mountain climbers to be used with down parkas. Foot sacks are always made of down. They fit kids up to the age of about six.

Still another solution is to put two kids together in one bag. Smaller children sometimes fit side by side in a normal rectangular bag. Two bigger kids can sleep comfortably at opposite ends of a rectangular bag, providing of course, the bag can be opened and closed at both ends.

Someone handy with a sewing machine can even make a down sleeping bag in a child's length from Frostline's do-it-yourself kit. The good feature of this kit is that, as the child grows, you can add on foot-long sections, thus increasing the bag's length right up to adult size. The do-it-yourselfer can also make down sleeping bags in adult sizes from kits by Frostline and Korikit. This is a less expensive way of getting a good down bag.

Bag Care

To paraphrase an old cliché, we firmly believe that if you take care of your sleeping bag, it will take care of you. A sleeping bag is warmer when the insulating material is all fluffed out. So, the first thing to do on reaching camp is to pull out your bag, spread it flat, and fluff it up. Repeat this procedure every morning.

The best way to store sleeping bags is to either hang them or lay them out full length in a dry place. The worst way is all rolled up in a stuff bag. If you do not have room to hang or lay the bag full length, store it loosely in a big cardboard box or in a chest of drawers. If your bag has wool or cotton in its construction and will be stored for a long period of time, a few moth balls are a wise precaution.

As we said earlier, bags with synthetic insulation can be dry-cleaned, but dry-cleaning is not recommended for down. Down bags can be washed, but this should not be done too often. Frequent airing—daily, if possible—in a sunny spot is also helpful in keeping sleeping bags clean. Only pure soaps or cleaners such as Woolite or Zero should be used to wash down sleeping bags. Detergents will wash the natural oils out of them. Use only warm water, never hot. Spot cleaning is preferable to complete washing, but there will come a day when the bag simply has to be fully washed. This can be done by hand in a tub, or in a front-loading, tumbler-type washer. Top-loading agitation washers compact the down too much and you will lose much of the loft and warmth. You may also loosen the baffles.

A down bag should not be picked up when soaking wet. The water inside may rip the baffles. Squeeze the water out gently with the palms of your hands. The bag can then be dried in a tumble-type dryer set at "warm," or in the open air. Even if the bag is machine dried, hang it out in the open air for a few days to make sure that it dries thoroughly.

One last tip. Keep all bags away from the fire. A spark on a nylon shell will melt a hole wide enough to stick your thumb in. Cotton and wool are flammable. If your bag gets wet, rely on the sun to dry it, not your campfire. In a pinch, propane or gas heaters, or even stoves can be brought into service, but be very careful.

The Blanket Roll

Modern sleeping bags have made the old-fashioned blanket roll an endangered species. Indeed, it may soon become extinct. There are many young campers, and by young we mean people under 50, who have never slept in one. But there is the odd old-timer, usually an old sheep herder or even camper, who has not abandoned the blanket roll. Such people may have given sleeping bags a try, but they probably bought cheap bags that wouldn't keep an Eskimo sled-dog warm in a heat wave. From this, they have concluded that sleeping bags are inferior to wool blankets and have stuck with the blankets.

There is no doubt that good wool blankets are warmer than a poor quality sleeping bag. In fact, for much of automobile and tent-trailer camping, sleeping bags are not essential. Blankets will do fine, and they are more versatile because they can be used at home. Because of this, blankets are a better bet for occasional campers. They are also a good bet for someone who is just getting into the camping game. It means that your initial investment in equipment can be kept low, just in case camping does not turn out to be your cup of tea. (Tyro campers should always begin their trysts with the outdoors in the balmy days of summer.)

The best blankets are the so-called Hudson Bay blankets of virgin wool. These are excellent, but expensive. In fact, you can easily buy two cheap sleepings bags for the price of one Hudson Bay blanket. Old army blankets are also quite good. Their wool, however, is harsher. Comforters of down, wool, or even synthetic insulation can also be used for automobile camping. In a pinch, so can cotton blankets or quilts during the summer months.

How do you make a blanket bed roll? Simple. Just lay one blanket over the other so that the top blanket overlaps the bottom over one half of its length, and the tops of the two blankets are about 6 inches apart. Then fold the top blanket in the middle along its entire length. Next fold the exposed half of the bottom blanket for its entire length over the folded top blanket. Now simply tuck the bottom under and your bed roll is finished. It has a double thickness of blanket on the top and bottom to keep the chill away from your back and front.

One Last Tip

When buying a sleeping bag, be sure to read all of the literature that comes with it. Don't just accept the word of a salesman. Any salesman can make an honest mistake in what he tells you, and there is always a chance that you can run into a man, the rotten apple in the barrel, who is eager to make a sale at any price. Do not hesitate to take your shoes and jacket off and crawl into the bag. See how it fits. See how much room it gives you to roll around. This is particularly important with mummy-type bags.

Consider renting. Again, this is a good bet for tyros who are not really sure whether they are going to like camping. Renting a sleeping bag is no different from renting a tent. The rented bags are mostly synthetically insulated so that they can be dry-cleaned.

CHAPTER 5

Cots and Mattresses—The Foundation of a Good Night's Sleep

The old bough bed of evergreen branches laid in a fish scale pattern is all but gone from the camping scene. We might even shed a tear or two for the modern camper who is unlikely to savor this experience. Somehow the fragrance of balsam and spruce branches epitomized the joys of camping. And contrary to the words of the current crop of camping writers, a bed of evergreen branches when correctly made of small twigs in a fish-scale pattern was quite comfortable, at least for the first few days until the branches settled down.

However, we cannot shed a tear for the practice of whacking off 50 or 60 branches needed to make such a bed. If every camper taking to the woods today were to do this, the forests in our more popular camping areas would have been denuded long ago. Yet there are places in the wilds of Canada where a camper can still make a bough bed without feeling guilty. There are places in Canada where a man seldom leaves a footprint or wets a paddle— even an Indian. If you are ever fortunate enough to visit such a place, make a bough bed and recapture a bit of the romance of old.

Sleeping on Air

The air mattress is still the work horse of camp beds. When properly inflated (not too full, just full enough to keep your hips about one inch off the ground), the air mattress makes a comfortable bed.

The best mattresses are made of a blended cloth of cotton and nylon, impregnated with rubber. This is the most durable material used in air-mattress construction. Air mattresses are also made of rubber and even plastic. Both materials are lighter than the rubber-impregnated cotton nylon. Plastic mattresses are very fragile and not even worthy of consideration by the serious camper.

Air mattresses generally come in two designs—those that have the tubes or baffles running lengthwise and those of a tufted design. The latter are superior. They are more comfortable but alas, they are also more expensive. Air mattresses come in various sizes. Seventy-five inches seems to be a

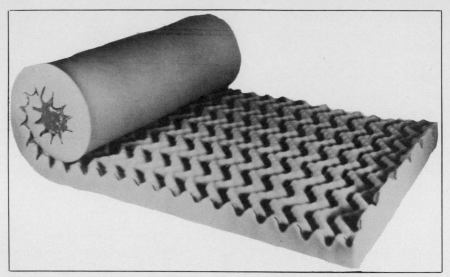

Foam mattresses have become very popular with many campers, and in many ways are more comfortable than air mattresses.

standard length, but widths range from 25 to 48 inches. There are also double-sized air mattresses of 64 inches or wider.

We feel that a mattress should be at least 32-inches wide and preferably 36-inches wide when inflated. A big man may need a 45-inch mattress if he thrashes about in his sleep. Note that we say "when inflated." Frequently the dimensions given on mattresses are those of the deflated mattress. You must take this into account.

There are also three-quarter length air mattresses on the market. These are generally about 45 inches in length. These mattresses are meant mostly for backpackers because they are a bit lighter. After trying them out, we feel that the full-length mattress is a better bet. With a short mattress, your legs dangle over the edge. Since a full length mattress weighs, on the average, only half a pound more than a three-quarter length one, we will stick to the full lengths.

One disadvantage of air mattresses is that they have to be inflated. When automobile camping, a pump can be carried for this task. However, if you are backpacking into the mountains or on a canoe trip with many portages, the pump means more weight and bulk. Blowing up air mattresses with lung power is a tedious task. At high altitudes it can leave the camper light-headed or even nauseous. Our only advice is to inflate the mattress slowly, in stages. There is no reason to go on a huffing and puffing marathon.

Here is a good tip. Always carry patching material with you in case your mattress gets a rupture. Be sure to have some patches of a fair size, at least the size of your palm. On the better mattresses the vent plugs are attached, but even they can tear off. If yours does, you can whittle a temporary substitute from a piece of soft wood.

You may have noticed that we have said nothing about air pillows, either as separate items or attached to air mattresses. Some people swear by them, but we swear at them. Our heads seem to slide every which way. In our minds, a sleeping bag stuff bag stuffed with a down jacket makes a better pillow, as do other rolled up articles of clothing. On an automobile camping trip, a down pillow is unbeatable.

Sleeping on Synthetics

Mattresses of synthetic foam have also become popular with many campers. Beds in tent trailers generally have foam mattresses. Foam mattresses have a waffled or ridged underside and a smooth top. Like air mattresses, they come in various widths and lengths. In many ways a foam mattress three inches thick is even more comfortable than an air mattress. The pores in the foam allow it to breathe in summer, so condensation is no problem. The biggest disadvantage of the foam mattress is its bulk, even when rolled up. Because of this, foam mattresses are suitable only for automobile camping or for tent trailers.

A more recent development in camping mattresses is the closed-cell polyutherane sleeping pad. These are generally known under trade names such as Poly-pad or Thermobar. They come in various thicknesses from ½ to 1½ inches. The thinner ones do nothing more than smooth out the bumps, while the 1½-inch pad is almost as comfortable as an air mattress. The insulating power of these pads is excellent.

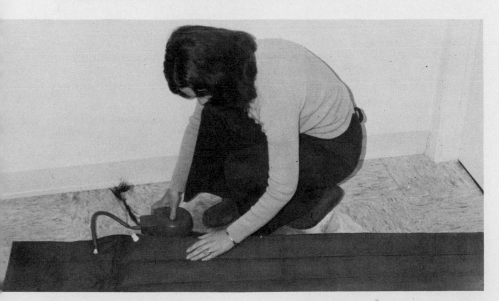

The air mattress is the workhorse of most camp beds. But be sure to check yours for leaks before heading out on the first camping trip of the year.

Being thinner than a foam mattress, they roll up into fairly compact bundles. Even the thicker pads are surprisingly light, not much heavier than some air mattresses. For example, Eddie Bauer's 1½-inch Poly-pad, measuring 6 x 2 feet, weighs only 50 ounces.

Closed-cell sleeping pads also come in various widths and lengths, including four-foot lengths for backpackers. We have found these four-foot sleeping pads to be very comfortable. Since the sleeper is only a little way off the ground, his legs do not dangle over the edge the way they do on a short air mattress. And certainly legs don't need padding.

We firmly believe that sleeping pads will in time become much more popular. They are not as heavy as many air mattresses and not much bulkier. In addition, you don't have to huff and puff when making your bed.

Sleeping on a Cot

Cots are frequently favored by women campers, particularly those who are not yet accustomed to the outdoors. Sometimes women are apprehensive about sleeping on the ground. Somehow they envision creatures creeping and crawling over them during the night, even in a tent with a sewn-in floor.

There are a number of camping cots on the market. One of the oldest and still the best is the old safari cot used by the U.S. Army. Its wooden legs are sturdy and its canvas is tough. But there are other cots, many with legs and frames of aluminum tubing for extra lightness. Some cots are designed to double as lounge chairs. One made by Lord Jim is a backpack frame that converts into a cot or a cot that converts into a backpack frame, whichever you prefer. These have the further versatility of doubling up as stowaway beds for guests at home.

Camp cots make the coolest beds during the hot summer months. Air circulates below them. But for cold-weather camping, they must be used with a mattress to insulate the sleeper.

Most camp cots are reasonably comfortable. We frequently use ours instead of air mattresses or sleeping pads during the summer. However, we are of the opinion that cots are not needed if the camper uses a mattress. Because of their bulk and weight, camping cots are not meant for the backpacker or the canoe tripper. Nor are they meant for sleeping in small tents with wedge-shaped roofs. Even in a large cottage tent, they take up a great deal of floor space.

If you decide to buy a camp cot, do not buy one sight unseen. Look it over carefully. Erect it and fold it a couple of times. Lie on it to see how comfortable and sturdy it is. Do not be afraid to wiggle it around. Roll around on it just as you would in your sleep. Your antics may gather a small audience, but that is a small price to pay if it will help you to buy a well made, sturdy cot instead of one of the flimsy contraptions that are on the market.

CHAPTER 6

Stoves by the Dozen

We are unabashed romantics when it comes to old traditions. One of these is cooking over a campfire. But we also pride ourselves in obeying the Ten Commandments of Camping, the first of which is "thou shall be pragmatic." Campfires, as pleasant as they are on chilly evenings, are not the most practical way to cook one's morning flapjacks. (Steaks on hickory coals are, of course, another matter, and constitute a separate chapter in this book.)

As far as cooking is concerned, modern camping has almost relegated the campfire to history books, to the writings of Nesmuk and Horace Kephard. Why? Because long ago we burned all of the wood in the more popular camping parks. Also, many of today's campers are urbanites who do not know how to make a good cooking fire. And we have yet to meet a woman who would rather cook over an open fire than on a modern camp stove. Campfires are hot on sultry summer days, miserable to cook on in the rain, and abominable in the wind. For camp cooking, stoves are in and campfires out—well, almost.

Which Stove to Choose?

Just before writing this chapter, we skimmed through the upper layer of a mass of camping-gear catalogs. Our brief look produced a count of some three dozen different camping stoves available, and we have not even scratched the proverbial top. Camping stoves can be divided into two classes—small ones for backpacking and large ones for automobile camping or more sedentary camping. A further division can be made on the basis of the fuel used—white gas, kerosene, butane, alcohol, propane, or wood.

Backpacking Stoves

Stoves for backpacking and canoe tripping come in a seemingly endless variety of models and designs. However, they are all small and light, and most of them are one-burner affairs. Although lightness is an important consideration, many backpackers carry this beyond rhyme or reason. It

The Coleman white gas, two-burner camp stove has been the most popular stove on the market for many years.

makes little sense to tear around from one sporting goods store to another in order to save one or two ounces on a stove, and then choose one for which the fuel comes in bulky, heavy containers.

Besides lightness, durability and compactness are two other important features. So are practicality of design, ease of use, and even safety. In our minds, however, one of the most important criteria is the fuel that the stove burns.

Kerosene burners   Kerosene has been the old standby fuel for campers for many years. It is less volatile than white gas and for this reason it is safer, which is why many campers prefer it. Another advantage of kerosene stoves is their dependability.

However, kerosene stoves are foul smelling and smoky appliances and for this reason they have lost much of their popularity. Also, kerosene is not

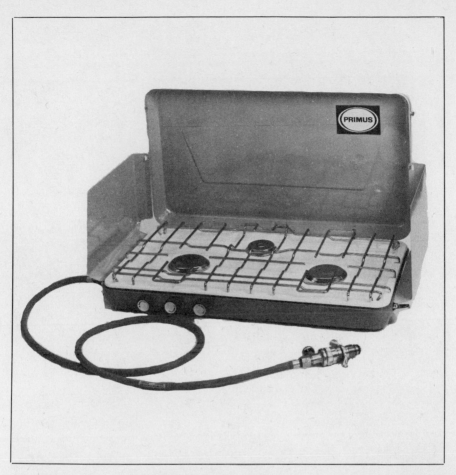

Propane camp stoves are rising in popularity very quickly because of their convenience, cleanliness, and high degree of safety.

always easy to obtain today. Yet the reverse is true in primitive areas here and abroad. And, of course, with a great deal of caution, other fuels such as white gas can be used.

Alcohol burners   The tiny little alcohol stoves are rarely encountered on today's camping scene, which is not surprising. They are just too inefficient and time consuming. Almost any other fuel will cook a meal in one third the time.

Sterno burners   The jelly-like substance known as Sterno was at one time quite popular as a fuel. The containers served as a burner and for this reason the product became known as "canned heat." However, since Sterno is alcoholic in base, the efficiency of it as a fuel is like that of alcohol, actually even a bit lower. The big selling feature of Sterno was its compactness, but that is about all it had going for it.

There are a number of small camp stoves on the market designed for the backpacker and canoe tripper. This one, the Svea 123, is one of the best.

Butane burners   Butane burners have become a fad among backpackers. Why, we don't know. In terms of energy—that is, heat—butane is far inferior to other fuels on a weight-by-weight basis. This means that you have to use much more of it to cook anything. Also it is many times more expensive than white gas.

Butane's efficiency at high altitudes declines even further. And at -24°C, about 15°F, you can forget about it altogether for cooking.

The popularity of butane is based largely on its convenience. It is easy to light. You don't have to worry about spills. And when a cartridge is empty, you simply slip in another. Butane also has a reputation for being very safe. Campers who will not use white gas don't hesitate to use butane. Alas, this sense of security is false. Puncture a butane cylinder with a spark-producing blow and, well, boom and goodbye. Another potential source of accidents is to change cylinders near a fire, should the cylinder you are taking out still have some gas in it.

Propane burners   Propane, in our opinion, is one of the best camping fuels. It is non-toxic and relatively safe. Although it is not as efficient at high altitudes and sub-zero temperatures as white gas, it is superior to butane. At sea level, campers prefer it to white gas or kerosene.

Propane stoves are light and compact, but unfortunately this is not true of the fuel cylinders or cartridges. However, if a comparison were made in terms of volume and weight versus burning time, propane would not compare badly at all. The problem with propane is that the cylinders are voluminous, giving more burning time than may be required.

White gas burners   As a fuel, white gas is one of the most efficient and one of the cleanest. Its major disadvantage is that it is fairly volatile.

There are a number of excellent and very efficient small camping stoves on the market that burn white gas. The best known brands are Primus, Optimus, and Svea, all of Swedish manufacture and all of excellent quality. Pick a stove that appeals to you and fits into your cooking kit.

The biggest problem with white gas stoves is that they function well only when the flame hole is kept meticulously clean. Follow the manufacturer's instructions on cleaning to the letter. We always clean the flame hole before lighting the stove. A little cleaning wire, protected in a clasp sheath, comes with each stove.

Another disadvantage of white gas stoves is that they work on self-created pressure. The heat above forces the white gas below up into the tube and turns it into a vapor which comes up the flame hole. Once the stove is lit, it works perfectly. The problem is to create the initial heat to begin vaporizing the gas so that the stove can be started. There are a number of ways of doing this. Clasping one's warm hands over the fuel tank is one. This works well in mildly cold weather, but forget it when it's really cold. Another way is to unscrew the filler cap and blow into the tank to drive some fuel up into the vaporizing tube. With most stoves you will have to hold them almost vertically and cock your head a little. You will also have to be careful or you'll get a mouthful of gas. A third method is to squirt two or three drops of fuel into the vaporizing tube with an eye dropper. You can either fill the eye dropper from the stove tank or from the spare fuel container. This is a good method if you do not lose or break the eye dropper. We carry a spare in a little plastic vial. The fourth method is one that we have never used; that is, starting a small flame in the depression of the burner head with alcohol. This sounds fine, but you must carry a small container of alcohol with you. When you buy a new stove, always try lighting it a few times before going out camping.

To keep the flame hole of a white gas burner clean, use only very finely filtered white gas meant specifically for camping appliances. Your local garage may sell white gas from barrels at a cheaper price than white gas in containers, but stay away from it. It is better to pay a little more and be sure of getting very clean fuel. You will not save much by buying fuel from bulk barrels, because you just don't use very much. Always use a small funnel with a fine mesh strainer when you pour white gas into the stove tank.

The best backpacking containers for white gas, or kerosene for that matter, are those made of spun aluminum. They are light and strong and have gasket tops that are leakproof.

One last tip about fuels: stick to the well known brands.

Camp stoves like this Browning pocket stove have been designed to burn a variety of fuels—kerosene, alcohol, sterno, butane, propane, and white gas.

Big Camping Stoves

The big two-burner or even three-burner camping stoves can also be divided into categories according to the fuel they burn—white gas or propane. White gas stoves are still the most popular, but propane is coming up fast.

We have already discussed the relative merits of the various fuels in our discourse on small backpacking stoves. White gas is still the most efficient fuel. It is also a little more economical than propane. But, in our opinion, the cleanliness and convenience of propane outweighs these considerations, and we have switched almost entirely to propane for our automobile and boat camping trips. Now we don't have any more blackened pots to clean or any messy fuels to pour. For automobile camping, the bulk and weight of the propane cylinders is not a great problem.

However, we do have a soft spot for the white gas stoves. Our old two-burner Coleman has served us for many years and is still good for many more to come. A camper who owns good and serviceable white gas appliances would be foolish to switch to propane just for the sake of changing. If we did not earn our living from writing on outdoor recreation, which necessitates that we try and test new equipment, we would not have changed either.

From the standpoint of capital investment, the two-burner stoves for white gas are still a little more economical than two-burner propane stoves of comparable quality. They are also a little cheaper to operate. Our experience has shown that with proper care white gas and propane stoves are equally durable. Both have long and useful lives. Both come with a variety of options and in several models.

All of the white gas, two-burner stoves fold down into compact cases. When erected, the sides and top serve as a wind break. When folded down, they protect the burners of the stove. Not all propane stoves have this feature. Almost equally important, not all propane stoves are easy to keep clean, although there are some models that are.

Both types of stoves come with optional folding stands which keep the stoves at waist level. Some of the older white gas stoves even have folding legs attached right to the sides. These folding stands are a good idea, but they tend to be a bit flimsy. A light folding table made of wooden slats is a bit more sturdy, offers more room for the cook, and is more versatile. Once the meal is cooked, you can put the stove on the ground and eat on the table.

There are a number of accessories available for these stoves. A thick aluminum griddle for frying eggs, pancakes, and fish, is one. A box-shaped oven that sits on top of one of the burners is another. Some of these ovens are collapsible for easy storage and transport. All have temperature gauges for cooks who are temperature conscious.

Wood stoves   Wood stoves have gone the way of the buffalo. They are not extinct, but seldom seen. They are too heavy and bulky even for an automobile camper with a big station wagon. And, of course, they require stovepipes. As we said earlier in this chapter, wood is becoming hard to get in many popular camping grounds.

Yet wood stoves are the favorites of professional outdoorsmen—the guides and outfitters in countless fishing and hunting camps in the forested wilderness. The fuel here is free for the taking. The wood stove is practical only in a semi-permanent camp that is pitched for the entire fishing or hunting season. The gear for these camps is generally hauled in on pack horses or, if the camp is in lake country, by pontoon-equipped aircraft. Once the camp is up, it stays up until the end of the operating season.

To us, there is nothing like a wood stove in a big wall tent to keep the fall chill away. In fact, a wood stove can keep a tent warm even in winter. And the meals that some camp cooks turn out on these stoves are among the best we have ever eaten.

The most practical wood-burning camp stoves we have seen are simple boxes of heavy sheet metal. The metal must be thick and heavy enough to stand hard knocks and not warp and buckle with heat. The dimensions of some of the more practical stoves are, roughly: 12-inches high, 16-inches wide, and 24-inches long. The door should be approximately 10 x 12 inches so that you can put in good chunks of wood, particularly at night when you want the fire to last. The latch on the door should be positive, and there should be an adjustable opening for drafts. The rear of the firebox should have an oven.

Porbably the best known and the best wood-burning camp stove is the old Sheepherder stove. It has been around for a long time, and we predict that it will remain on the scene for many years to come, as long as fishermen and hunters make forays into the mountain country of the west. May that be forever!

Wood Stove Safety

A camper today will use a wood-burning camp stove only in a wilderness camp put up by an outfitter. The first rule is to feed the stove sparingly. Adjust the draft dampers so that you allow in just enough air. Too much wood and too much of a draft will cause a roaring fire that may ignite the tent. Besides being dangerous, such a fire is too hot to cook on and may buckle the stove or its sides. Very hot fires will shorten the life of a thin metal stove.

The outfitter will have the stove set up. In fact, every tent may have a stove. There may also be an additional stove outside for cooking in hot weather. But if you have to set up a wood-burning stove yourself, here are a few hints. The stove should not be closer than two feet away from the tent wall; three feet is better. The heat of a stove can set a tent wall on fire. Be sure to have a metal or, better still, an asbestos collar around the stovepipe where it protrudes through the tent wall. This collar should have a bit of

There is a revived interest in the art of cooking over a campfire, even though most campers have camp stoves with them.

leeway—three inches or so—on either side of the tent fabric to allow for movement during strong winds.

Ideally the stove should sit in a bed of sand that is about three or four inches deep and six inches wider on all sides than the stove. A sheet of asbestos may be used instead of sand. The outside stovepipe should be a foot away from the tent wall, but a bit more is even better. Be sure that it is attached firmly to a solid post so that strong winds won't blow it off and knock it against the fabric of the tent. Have a spark stopper, such as a piece of fine wire screen, on top of the pipe to keep sparks from flying on to your tent or into the bush.

CHAPTER 7

Equipping the Galley

Most women have more dishes in their home kitchens than they need. Proof of this is the camp kitchen. Superb camp meals are turned out with comparatively few dishes, sometimes with only one pot. So keep your repertoire of pots, pans, and eating utensils down to the essentials.

The Kitchen Kit

Most campers begin their outdoors kitchen kit by dragging out a few old dishes from home. We did. And if your camping is confined to a tent trailer with a lot of cupboard space, that's fine. You do not have to be too concerned about space, but leave old, breakable crockery at home and buy some of the synthetic unbreakables, and that includes tumblers for drinking.

Undisputably, the handiest type of cook kit is the kind where the pieces nestle or stack into one another to form a compact bundle. The beauty of such a kit is its versatility. It can be used for all kinds of camping from backpacking to trailer tenting. The only criticism of the nesting kit that can be raised is that the dishes are designed with utility and compactness in mind, rather than convenience, which makes some of them slightly awkward to use.

There are a number of such kits on the market, ranging in size to accommodate from one to six-man parties. Some of the cook kits are fairly spartan. Others are designed so that a backpacker's stove, such as the Svea 123, fits right inside. These kits even include a wind screen for the stove.

Hikers on a limited budget can make a surprisingly effective cook kit from coffee cans. If you get cans in sizes from one to three pounds, you will see that they fit into each other. Pliers can be used for handles. Add a small steel skillet to three cans, and you are set. This, by the way, is not our idea. We got it from a couple of teenage kids that we met while canoeing on a wild river in northern Ontario.

Most of us, however, prefer to use store-bought cook kits. The most practical ones are made by such outfits as Smilie and Sigg. Smilie, in particular, has a wide selection of wares for the camp galley.

The handiest type of cook kit is the kind where the dishes nestle or stack into one another to form a compact bundle.

Here is our basic cook kit, based on four people in the party:

—One pot, 8 quarts.	Serves as a water bucket, wash-up pail, and stew pot.
—One pot, 4 quarts.	Used for cooking staple starches.
—One pot, 2 quarts.	Used for cooking meat and soup.
—One coffee pot, 2 quarts.	If instant coffee is used, you can substitute a 1-quart kettle.
—Two steel skillets, 9 inches.	Note that we said steel. More on this later.

The two smaller kettles should have flat lids so that while one kettle is on the stove, the other can sit on top of it and be kept warm. One two-burner stove or two one-burner stoves will be needed to cook for a party of four people.

As for a basic mess kit, four plates, four cups, and four sets of knives, forks, and spoons are adequate. Remember that we are discussing basic kits here. For an arduous backpacking trip, these kits could be pared down a bit more. One frying pan could be left behind. So could the coffee pot if everyone used instant coffee or tea bags. The knives could be eliminated as well. We never take ours. We use our sheath or folding knives instead. Certainly every member of a backpacking or canoe tripping party should have his or her folding or sheath knife with him.

On the other hand, on an automobile camping trip, these kitchen kits could be expanded. A plastic water pail and a wash basin for dishes are handy. Bowls for soup or canned fruit can also be included, as can dessert spoons. Otherwise, everyone simply licks off his or her big spoon or fork.

In the case of a two-person party, the 8-quart kettle and one frying pan can be scrapped, and the number of cups and plates halved. On the other hand, for a six-man party, another 4-quart pot will be needed and two pots would be even better. The number of spoons, forks, cups, and plates will have to come up as well.

Before we go on to describe additional items that can be included, let's have a word about skillets. There is no doubt that cast iron, and the thicker the better, is the best bet for skillets. But it is brutally heavy. For automobile camping, a cast-iron skillet is unbeatable. It heats up slowly but it retains its heat very well. However, its biggest virtue is that it gives off heat uniformly. The steel skillet is the next best and it is much lighter. It is certainly light enough for a backpacker to use, at least on some trips. The last choice is aluminum. It flares up quickly and if the heat source is variable, so is the heat of the aluminum skillet.

Here is a cook kit that will serve the needs of four people quite amply.

The Rest of the Cooking Kit

In addition to the basics, there are a number of other items you can bring along in the cooking kit to make cooking a bit easier and more varied.

The *reflector oven* is a handy item for baking anything from cookies to fish. All reflector ovens fold down flat for traveling and are very light. On a long camping trip, a reflector oven is a real boon. It really helps to add variety to the menu. And with so many cookie, cake, and other mixes on the market today, baking is not the chore it used to be. Whenever we can, we take our oven along. It requires a wood fire.

The man who invented the *Dutch oven* was a genius. It is one of the most useful and versatile cooking utensils ever designed. It is simply a thick-walled pot with three stubby legs and a tightly fitting lid with a high rim. The high rim on the lid is designed to hold hot coals and the legs on the pot allow hot coals to be shoveled under the Dutch oven.

A Dutch oven can be used for boiling, frying, or baking. It is ideal for one-pot meals such as stews. Just put the fixings into the pot and bury it in hot coals. When you return at the end of the day, your dinner will be cooked. Old lumberjack-style baked beans turn out their best when cooked in a Dutch oven. And, as if the Dutch oven did not have enough talents already, it bakes the finest bread and biscuits we have ever tasted.

What makes the Dutch oven so unique is that it heats up slowly and retains its heat for a long time, thereby cooking steadily and evenly. Even without too much attention, a burned meal is a rarity because of the even heat. Alas, these remarks apply only to Dutch ovens made of cast iron. Aluminum ovens are not as good.

The only disadvantage of the Dutch oven is its weight and bulk. It was not meant for backpackers. The aluminum Dutch ovens are quite light in weight, but as we have said, they heat up quickly and cool off just as quickly.

The *grate* or *grill* can be a very useful implement if you are going to cook over an open fire or barbecue. Many of the folding backpacker grills are useless for barbecuing because the crossbars are too widely spaced.

There are various sizes of grates on the market. We feel that the minimum size for a useful grate is about 18 by 12 inches. One that we like is made by Cassidy Products. It disassembles into a two-piece tube, with the tube acting as an outside frame when the grill is in use.

The *griddle* is another useful cooking utensil, particularly for fish, steak, or eggs. If you will be cooking over an open fire, a thick iron griddle is the best. Aluminum griddles have the same deficiencies as aluminum Dutch ovens. Their lightness is their only advantage.

When the source of heat is constant, such as from a two-burner camping stove, an aluminim griddle becomes much more efficient. It will heat up quickly and, as long as the flame remains constant, so will the griddle.

A grate or grill is extremely useful if you are going to barbecue or cook over an open fire. This one, by Cassidy Products, disassembles into a compact tube.

Many barbecue fans are taking to the camping scene with light, portable, charcoal *barbecue grills*. There are a number of these on the market, and the idea is fine if you have room to carry it. A very satisfactory barbecue grill can be made by digging a pit, about three inches deep, into the ground. Line it with aluminum foil and put in the charcoal. Four rocks or forked sticks are then used to hold up the grate on all four corners.

There are also several portable propane barbecue grills on the market. These again are fine if you have room to take them with you, but they are not an indispensable item on a camping trip.

Miscellaneous Utensils

A spatula is almost indispensable. Backpackers will find plastic lighter, but even the metal ones are not heavy. A big ladle is also useful where there are a number of campers and lots of soups or stews are cooked. A big fork can be useful, but not essential, as are kitchen tongs.

A thin-bladed kitchen knife is better than most sheath knives for slicing or filleting fish. On a backpacking trip you can do without it, but on an automobile camping trip you can easily have two. Aside from this, you will need a can opener and a bottle opener. A roll of tinfoil is another handy item. Most campers use it for baking potatoes in the campfire coals. If you have to, you can even cook several entire meals on utensils fashioned from tinfoil. You can build a reflector oven from foil, like a miniature lean-to.

For dishwashing, a small plastic bottle of detergent and a copper or plastic scouring pad along with a dish towel are musts. Scouring pads are better than grass, moss, or sand any day.

The Grub Box

Dishes and grub have to be packed somewhere. With tent trailers and other recreational vehicles, there is usually enough cupboard space that where to put the dishes seldom becomes a problem.

One of the best ways to transport food and camping dishes on an automobile camping trip is in a sturdy plywood box made for this purpose. Almost any do-it-yourselfer can come up with a grub box designed to suit his camping needs.

A good type of box is one where the bottom has slots for leather or web straps that can be used to strap the box around a tree so that the box hangs about chest high. The lid of the opened box can serve as a handy platform for many chores once the box has been attached to a tree.

Some campers store and transport their dishes and grub in an old, but sturdy suitcase. All they have to do is run a quick inventory and make certain that everything is there and that their dishes are ready to go. Most of us have battered and shabby suitcases that could serve for this purpose.

Backpackers, of course, do not have this advantage. They must repack their backpacks.

CHAPTER 8

Keeping Things Cool

Keeping perishable foods from spoiling has always been a problem for campers. To a degree, it is still a problem. Modern campers, however, have several advantages over those of yesteryear. Not only has modern technology produced an excellent selection of nutritious and flavorful freeze-dried foods for the backpacker and canoe camper, but it has also developed a number of efficient coolers and refrigerators for the automobile camper.

Camp Refrigerators

Many campers think that portable refrigerators (real refrigerators, not coolers or iceboxes) are a new idea. They are not. Well equipped African safari camps have been using kerosene-burning refrigerators for 30 years or more. However, camping refrigerators did not become popular until the advent of camping trailers and tent trailers. Today, nearly all camping trailers and nearly all of the more luxurious tent trailers come equipped with small refrigerators. These are usually propane operated, but many have two power sources, propane and electricity. A few of these refrigerators even allow the use of a 12-volt battery as a power source if you run out of propane and the campground has no electric plug-ins.

Most refrigerators in tent or camping trailers are built in. In a few cases, however, they are portable, thus allowing the refrigerator to be taken on a boat or into a station wagon. Certainly, a portable refrigerator is a much more versatile appliance than a stationary one. For example, a couple we know use theirs at home, keeping beer and soft drinks cold in it under the bar in their rec room.

There is no doubt that refrigerators are more efficient at preserving perishable foods than ice-cooled coolers. They are also more convenient. But this efficiency and convenience cost money. A two-cubic foot camping refrigerator costs about $190, while a 3.5-cubic foot unit runs about $250.

It is difficult to make a capacity comparison between coolers and camping refrigerators. Not only because the capacity of coolers is given in quarts and that of refrigerators in cubic feet, but also because part of the space in the cooler must be occupied by ice. The more ice, the less storage space, but the greater the cooling effect. Weightwise, refrigerators weigh about the same as coolers containing 25 pounds of ice. A small refrigerator will hold as much food as a big cooler because no space is taken up by the cooling ice.

Camp Coolers

There is such an array of coolers or ice chests on the market today that selecting the right one can be a baffling task. The best and most expensive coolers have all-metal exteriors, either enameled steel or aluminum. Their entire bodies, including the lids, are fully insulated and there are double gaskets around the lid to keep warm air out. The lids close tightly with a metal latch. The handles on the sides are recessed, as is the drain spout on the bottom, so that they will not accidentally be ripped or knocked off.

The next in line are coolers made entirely of high density plastic. These are surprisingly rugged, but on many models the lids are not insulated and they generally close only a fraction as tightly as the metal ones. Usually the ice has to be replenished more frequently in plastic coolers.

The insulation in both types of coolers is urethane foam, while the interior is made of molded plastic that is easy to clean. Surprisingly, the high density plastic is as heavy as metal.

The cheapest is the so-called styrofoam cooler made of expanded polystyrene foam. The insulating qualities of this type of cooler are not high. They may be suitable for a country picnic or a day at the beach, but not for an extended camping trip. They are also too fragile to last long and heavy loads of ice and food cannot be kept in them. Because of their flimsy nature they are quite easily crushed, particularly the lids.

Chest-type coolers are by far the most common, but there are models on the market that can be used as uprights. This also applies to small refrigerators. We recommend the chest-type cooler because the cold air inside tends to be compressed by the warmer air outside, thus you do not get the inflow of warm air every time you open the cooler.

Many coolers come with a variety of options. Trays that keep the food above and out of the water from melting ice are a good bet. A separate ice tub is another useful feature. A water jug is also good. You can fill the water jug and freeze it at home, then you have ice for the first leg of your trip. We use empty bleach gallons for this purpose. We wash them and fill them, leaving enough headroom for the freezing water to expand. Once the water in the jug is frozen, we place it in the bottom of the cooler. As the ice melts, the water can be drained off and used for cold drinks, and the bottom of the cooler remains relatively dry.

Our preference is for metal coolers because they can also be used as seats in camp. Indeed, some models even come with lids that are padded on the top. But regardless of the type of cooler you buy, be sure that the interior is in one piece and that the corners are rounded for easy cleaning. The hinges on coolers with metal exteriors should be made of stainless steel or a similar non-rusting material.

There is a wide array of coolers or ice chests on the market today. The best have all-metal exteriors, but those of high density plastics are good as well. The chest-types are superior to the upright models.

One last tip about choosing a cooler. Buy the largest one that will fit into your car or tent trailer. There never seems to be enough room for all of the perishables, and the big coolers allow you to use bigger chunks of ice.

Using Your Cooler

Block ice is the most efficient way of keeping a cooler cool. Ice cubes melt far too quickly. It is amazing, though, just how quickly a 20-pound block of ice will melt if care is not taken to preserve it. The contents of your ice chest will keep cooler if you open it as seldom as possible and if you close it as quickly as possible before all of the cold air escapes. For this reason, some campers use two ice chests—the main cooler is opened only in the morning and all of the essential items for the day are taken out and put into the smaller auxiliary cooler where they are used as needed.

If you drain off water from your cooler, be certain to close the spigot tightly to prevent warm air from traveling up the drain hole into the cooler.

Before departing on your trip, pre-chill all of the items in your home refrigerator and even freeze your meat before putting it in. In this way the contents of the ice chest will be cold when you put it in, and it will not release any warmth to melt the ice. However, make certain that the frozen items are well wrapped in plastic to keep them away from melting ice.

Also, keep your ice chest away from sunlight. In camp, leave it in a shady spot. Cover it with a sleeping bag or a blanket if necessary. Avoid leaving it on sand or rocks that heat up quickly and retain their heat well into the evening.

Finally, do not feel compelled to refrigerate everything that you normally refrigerate at home. Butter or margarine will keep for a fair amount of time unrefrigerated if stored in a plastic container. So will jams and such items as honey and peanut butter. Cheese, wrapped in individual air-tight wrappers, will also keep for a surprisingly long time without refrigeration. Instead of cold cuts, use dry salamis and sausages that need little or no refrigeration. In this way, you can save space for those food items which truly must be refrigerated.

Portable refrigerators for camping are not really new, but they did not become popular until the advent of camping trailers and tent trailers.

The white-gas camping lantern is an old standard. Coleman makes the only white gas lanterns and they have become famous all over the world.

CHAPTER 9

Let There Be Light

It was dusk and we were just finishing our second cup of coffee when a tent trailer pulled into the campsite next to us. The first thing our new neighbors did was to rig up three lanterns, all of them big two-mantle jobs, around the campsite. They then began to erect their tent. The campsite glowed like a gigantic bonfire. The lights stayed up until they went to bed some three hours later.

The glare of the lights bothered us at first, but we made the best of it by turning our backs to our neighbors. What bothered us even more was the spirit of our neighbors. We sat and talked, watching the night sky as it became studded by millions of starry diamonds. Later the aurora borealis began to pull her wispy, mysterious drapes of light across the northern sky. It was a dazzling light show, the kind that city dwellers never see. Our neighbors missed it all.

Why do such people go camping, we wondered. We still wonder. These people used a typical American overkill—a sledge hammer where a tack hammer would do. Lights of some sort are a must on every camping trip— to cook a late meal, to perform some late chores, or perhaps to do a bit of reading. But the glaring light of camping lanterns kills your night vision, and there are times when a light detracts from the environment around you.

Lanterns by the Dozen

There are many models of lanterns on the market today. We have already discussed fuels at some length in the chapter on stoves, so there is no need for us to go into their pros and cons again.

Kerosene lanterns are still with us, but they are seldom used in camping. They do not give much light but their fuel lasts a long time. We recommend kerosene lanterns only if you are still using a kerosene stove. Kerosene lanterns are used mainly in summer cabins or cottages and by trappers and Indians living in the bush.

White gas lanterns are probably still the most widely used light source. However, propane is coming up fast. Coleman is the only maker of white gas camping lanterns, and Coleman lanterns have become justly famous.

There has been a fair amount of emphasis placed on the dangers of white gas appliances. While we do not want to minimize the potential danger, we do believe that these appliances are not really any more dangerous than machines such as gasoline-powered lawn mowers. White gas appliances should never be refueled in a tent. And, of course, they should never be refueled while they are in operation or near a fire or by a camper smoking a cigarette.

Any camper who follows the maker's instructions will be rewarded by long and safe service. We have been. White gas lanterns are cheaper to operate than lanterns of any other fuel type. But perhaps even more

There is a large number of propane camping lanterns on the market, such as this one by Primus. Others are made by Coleman, Garcia, Zebco, Paulin, and Trailblazer.

important, they are fully portable. This is not always true of propane lanterns when a bulk tank is used.

We feel that the one-mantle Coleman lantern is adequate for most purposes. An automobile camper is better off buying two one-mantle lanterns than one two-mantle. The two smaller lanterns will give more light than one bigger one, and they can also be more strategically located. In addition, you have an extra lantern, a spare at all times.

Propane appliances, including lanterns, have become very popular in recent years. There is no doubt that propane is a cleaner fuel and more convenient because the cylinders do not have to be pumped up. Propane lanterns can be had with disposable cylinders (something we are against; the world does not need any more disposables), but they can also be coupled to refillable bulk tanks. Ideally campers should have all of their appliances standardized—either all propane or all white gas.

Propane lanterns are made by Coleman, Primus, Garcia, Trailblazer-by-Winchester, Zebco, Paulin, and possibly others. There is a tremendous variety. We recommend only those models that can be used with bulk tanks. Propane lanterns with cylinders and small tanks are as portable as white gas lanterns, but this is generally not the case when they are attached to a bulk tank to which the stove or some other appliance may also be attached.

Only you can decide what wattage output you need, but generally an output of 100 to 150 watts is adequate for most conditions. The advantage of propane lanterns is that the light output can easily be controlled by regulating the flow of fuel. Again we feel that two one-mantle lanterns are more versatile than a big two-mantle.

Propane lanterns come in a variety of weights. This can be an important feature for a backpacker or canoe tripper. For example, the Primus Explorer No. 2220 and the Garcia L-200 are of the same light output, but the Primus lantern is almost one pound lighter. It pays to look around and be very selective.

Both white gas and propane lanterns come with globes of clear or frosted glass. We like the frosted globes because they cut down on harsh, glaring light. They both come with a variety of optional features and gadgets such as stands, hooks for hanging, reflectors, and holders. You may find some of these items useful, so investigate them thoroughly.

Some propane lanterns are more automated. The Trailblazer-by-Winchester, for example, has "no match" models which light themselves when they are turned on. This has been hailed as a great innovation.

While on the subject of propane lanterns, some of the European-made lanterns such as the Primus need a special adaptor when they are being attached to refillable bulk tanks. This does not present any sort of handicap, but you should be aware of it. Both propane and white gas lanterns throw a fair amount of heat. If they are hung too close to the tent roof, they may scorch or even burn the fabric. They should not be hung on trees near leaves because they could kill the leaves by drying them out.

Butane lanterns are also available. We have a better opinion of butane lanterns than of butane stoves. Butane lanterns are much more efficient, but some of the bugs of butane still exist. It's not very good fuel for high altitudes or for cold weather because, below 32 degrees Fahrenheit, butane will not vaporize. Butane is also a very expensive fuel, more costly than propane and much more costly than white gas. Butane lanterns, like butane stoves, are fed from disposable cartridges or cylinders, and we have already stated our opinion of disposables.

Butane lanterns are a reasonably good bet for the backpacker, the canoe tripper, or the bike camper, should these campers feel that they need a lantern. Butane lanterns are certainly more compact and lighter than propane lanterns and much more compact than white gas lanterns.

Before leaving the subject of lanterns, we would like to ask you a question. Do you really need a lantern? Backpackers and canoe trippers have shown that lanterns are not an essential piece of camping equipment. They have proved that a flashlight is the only source of light needed. We have certainly made a number of canoe trips without burdening ourselves with a lantern and fuel. On the other hand, an automobile camper should take along a lantern or two. The weight and bulk do not matter much to him. However, a lantern and fuel are not enough. Lanterns get jostled on every camping trip. Shattered globes and broken mantles are quite common, so take a spare globe and several mantles along as well.

Only Trailblazer-by-Winchester and Coleman offer carrying cases for their lanterns. Coleman's case is metal, while Trailblazer's is molded polystyrene. A do-it-yourselfer can make a case out of plywood, while a little electric tape and a couple of coats of varnish will reinforce the paper carton that the lantern was purchased in to make a perfectly satisfactory case. Lanterns should be stored somewhere to protect them from breakage during travel. The Garcia propane lantern No. L-400 is an ingenious piece of design work. The lantern body acts as a case for traveling. The globe fits inside the base.

Lighting with Electricity

A flashlight is a must on any camping trip. We certainly would not go camping without one. The flashlight need not be extremely powerful; one that takes two medium-sized batteries is quite adequate. All you need it for is to check on the kids or to find your way if nature beckons in the middle of the night. The main thing is to buy a flashlight of good quality. The cheap, junky ones never last. Backpackers will find the Mallory Compact a good bet. Complete with two batteries, it weighs only 6 ounces.

Car campers should carry with them a light that incorporates a red blinker. There are a number of these on the market. Boat campers will find the Ray-O-Vac No. L400 handy. It floats and is virtually rustproof. A flashlight for a car or boat camper should be powered by a heavy-duty battery.

Some campers are now using fluorescent lights instead of lanterns to illuminate their campsites. There are a number of these on the market—

A number of manufacturers such as Coleman and Trailblazer make carrying cases for their lanterns. These are a good idea because broken globes and mantles are common on unprotected lanterns.

some powered by battery only, others by battery or 110-volt AC current, and Coleman's Charger 3000 which is rechargeable and can be used on either 12-volt battery or 110-volt AC. The cost of these fluorescent lights ranges from $30 to $60 depending on the features and construction. There are also cheaper fluorescent lights on the market that plug into the cigarette lighter socket in your car. These are available mainly in automotive supply shops.

One Last Tip

Every camper should carry with him two or three candles as an auxiliary light source. This is particularly true for backpackers and canoe trippers. The slow burning, non-drip candles are superior to the ones of ordinary paraffin wax. They are available from outfitters specializing in backpacking gear. For extra safety, ideally the candles should be used in a metal candle lantern. There are a number of these on the market, all of them compact, light, and windproof.

A candle has uses beyond lighting. On a wet day it makes a handy fire starter. The paraffin can also be used for waterproofing a small leak along the seams of the tent.

CHAPTER 10

Tools of the Trade

Every outdoor activity requires that the participant be properly equipped. The angler needs a fishing rod and reel, lures, plus perhaps boots or waders. The hunter needs an appropriate shotgun or rifle. Even the bird watcher should have a pair of binoculars and a bird-identification guide.

The camper is no exception. We all know this. He needs a long list of equipment and we have already described much of it in the preceeding chapters. Items such as tents, sleeping bags, pads or mattresses, stoves, lanterns, coolers, pots and pans, and other equipment for the galley are all necessary. Then, of course, there are specialized pieces of equipment— backpacks, canoes, snowshoes and the like—for special types of camping. In addition, the camper also needs some of the basic fundamental tools of the outdoorsman.

In our opinion, every camper on a wilderness trip should have a knife. That applies for women as well, but not of course for young children. On an automobile camping trip, a knife should be taken along whenever you are venturing into the bush, even if it is only to pick blueberries up on the ridge. With a good knife in a pocket or sheath, an outdoorsman or outdoorswoman is never helpless, even if lost in the wilds.

The Vital Knife

The knife is one of man's first tools. It began as nothing more than a sharp piece of stone with which our early ancestors cut the skin and flesh from animals they killed or carrion they picked up. The knife did not become a weapon until the Late Stone Age or perhaps even the Bronze Age. Until that time, it was not efficient enough.

An ax and a saw are two very useful camping tools. Axmanship is still synonymous with woodsmanship in remote areas. But a Swede saw is a better bet for bucking up firewood.

Time and technology may have changed the knife's appearance, but they have not changed its use. To an outdoorsman, it is indispensable. Outdoorsmen's knives can be divided into two broad categories—sheath knives and folding knives. These terms are quite descriptive. In the case of folding knives, the blade folds into the handle, while a sheath knife is carried in a sheath, usually on the belt.

Sheath knives come in a variety of styles for a variety of purposes ranging from knives with long, thin, flexible blades designed especially for filleting fish, to the Eskimo oo-you, a skinning knife made with a semi-circular blade. On the other hand, folding knives are general-purpose knives, with the size determining the purpose, as for example small pen knives.

Choosing a knife is not at all difficult once you have decided on its purpose. Other criteria, such as personal preference in style and design may also be important. Cost may be another consideration. But the overriding factor should be quality. A knife should be thought of as an investment. A good knife is a good investment. If properly taken care of, it will last for many years, even a lifetime.

Good knives are never cheap. But even a good knife can be purchased for a modest sum if you do not want a one-of-a-kind item wrought by a custom knifemaker. Only knife collectors concern themselves with the fine points of how knives are made, how the blades are forged and tempered, and what type of steel is used in the blade. All a camper needs to know is how to spot good quality. This is not always easy to detect in knives, but here are a few hints.

With sheath knives, look at the way the handle is attached to the blade. Bolt rivets running through the handle are an excellent way of attaching the handle firmly. A bolt that is part of the knife blade is also good. Beware of any embellishment on the blade. It has no function in cutting, and may have been put on the knife to distract the purchaser from flaws or poor quality. There should be no gaps where the guard meets the blade. The finish should shine. The lines should be clean and smooth. The knife should look and feel solid, even if it is very delicately bladed.

One key to good knife quality lies in the sheath. Any maker or manufacturer of good knives will not supply sheaths of poor workmanship or quality. However, not all sheaths of quality knives are practical for field use. When you see what appears to be a good quality knife in a cheap and shoddy sheath, stay away from it.

Picking a good quality folding knife is sometimes a little easier. Look for a smooth spring action when the knife is opened and closed. The blade should audibly click into the open and closed positions. When a folding knife is closed the point of its blade should be covered by the sides of the handle. When the knife is opened the blade should not shimmy from side to side. Such movement indicates a loose pivot rivet. The handle, or rather the covering on a folding knife's body that serves as a handle, should be firmly attached. If it looks rather flimsy stay away from it.

One of the most dependable and easiest ways of insuring that the knife

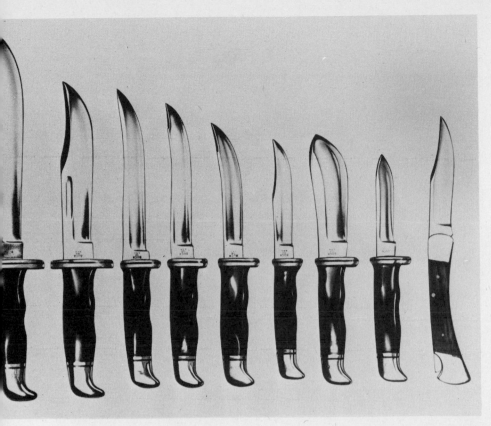

Probably the most useful tool a camper can have is a good knife, either in his pocket or in a sheath on his belt.

you buy is a good one is to purchase knives made by well-known knifemakers. Basically there are four classes of knifemakers. The first are custom knifesmiths. These men make knives entirely by hand, sometimes putting up to 12 hours of highly skilled hand labor into a knife with special features. Needless to say, custom knives are expensive but, in our opinion, they are well worth the investment for an outdoorsman who uses his knife regularly. A good, general use, custom-made outdoor knife by a top knifesmith can be purchased even today for about $50. Top custom knifemakers are Randall, Moran, Draper, Boone, Cooper, Hibben, Loveless, Morseth, Seguine, and Carey. A comprehensive list of knifemakers and their addresses can be obtained from A. G. Russell, P.O. Box 474, Fayetteville, Arkansas 72701.

The second-best group of outdoor knives are those made by production manufacturing techniques. Their prices are, of course, lower, but the knives are also of good quality. Buck, Olsen, Gerber, Browning, Colt, and Puma

Folding knives, sometimes called pocket knives, are general purpose knives, well suited for many camping chores.

are well-known makers of such knives. Prices range from about $15 for smaller models to about $45. It is surprising that companies such as Gerber and Buck can turn out knives of such good quality at such comparatively low prices.

The third-best class are knives that are truly mass produced, yet good quality is still maintained. Such knives range in price from about $10 to $15. They are a good buy for a man who feels that this is all he can afford. Respected brand names are Marble, Case, Western, Schrade-Walden, and Normark.

Custom knifemakers carefully inspect their knives during every stage of manufacture. Mass producers, on the other hand, cannot maintain as rigid a quality control. Thus in mass production knives, it is at times possible to buy one that has slipped through quality control. When this happens, you can pretty well count on the manufacturer to give you a replacement. Manufacturers stand behind their products, which is something that the manufacturers of very cheap knives, the fourth class of knife makers, never do. If they did, they could not stay in business for very long.

Which Knife for What Purpose

As we stated earlier, the choice of an outdoor knife depends on its purpose. A camper will find a knife with a 3-inch blade ample for almost all tasks.

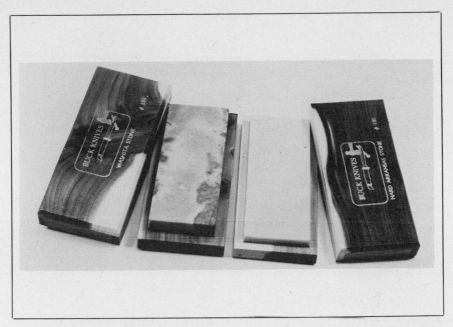

A dull knife is dangerous because it can slip. It is also useless. Good medium and fine oil stones are needed to keep knives sharp.

Such a knife will be useful for most chores around camp. A 3-inch blade is long enough for making a fire stick from a dry white pine bough, for most cutting jobs around camp, for dressing out a game bird, or for cleaning a fish—even a 20-pound northern pike.

The camper can choose either a sheath or a folding knife, depending on personal preference. There are several fine folding knives on the market with blades of that length. However, one of the problems with folding knives is that they are generally carried in the pocket where they can be lost easily. Also, the sturdier and heavier folding knives are too heavy and bulky to make ideal pocket knives. For this reason, some folding knives do come with a belt case, and this is a great idea.

Another general outdoor knife is one with a 4-inch or a 4½-inch blade. Such a knife is a bit more versatile. It will perform almost anything that the smaller blade knife will, and then some. You may feel a bit foolish dressing out an 8-inch brook trout with such a big knife but, on the other hand, a 4½-inch blade is long enough for filleting a 15-pound lake trout. If you are a hunter, a 4½-inch knife is a better bet for dressing out a moose or an elk. A 3-inch blade will do the job, but it is easier with the bigger blade. In fact, for dressing large big-game animals, a 5-inch blade may be even better. However, in our opinion, a blade longer than 5 inches is never needed. Any experienced woodsman will tell you that the mark of a greenhorn is a long-bladed knife.

Campers who are also serious fishermen may want a filleting knife. Although the flesh of fish is relatively soft and easy to cut, a filleting knife must be able to take and hold a sharp edge. Filleting fish is actually quite delicate work.

Keeping a Knife Sharp

A dull knife is not much use, and it is also dangerous. When a knife is dull, more strength has to be exerted to make it cut. This can cause it to slip, and a cut with a dull knife is more hazardous than one with a sharp knife because a dull knife tends to tear a wound, destroying more cells and making a much wider gash that takes longer to heal. The cut of a sharp knife is finer. Less tissue is destroyed, the cut does not bleed as much, it heals faster, and is less prone to infection. A knife that is properly cared for is never allowed to become too dull. A very dull knife is much harder to sharpen than one that is slightly or moderately dull and the edge can get ruined much more quickly.

Sharpening a knife is not a difficult task. A knife with a hard blade may take longer to sharpen, but it stays sharp longer. The knife with a soft blade sharpens quickly and becomes dull just as quickly. A soft blade is a mark of a cheap knife.

There are two considerations to take into account when sharpening a knife. First, are you just touching up the edge or, second, are you putting on a new edge? The latter should be done on a table, bench, or some other firm support, and with a big oilstone. Touching up can be done in the field and usually with a small pocket stone.

To sharpen a knife, lift the back of the blade so that the blade is at a 20-degree angle. Now stroke the blade across the stone from the back to the point, first on one side and then on the other. Bear down on the knife with some force, but make sure that you maintain the 20-degree angle. Light strokes will not achieve much. When the edge no longer reflects light and you can shave a hair off your arm, you know that your knife is sharp. Buck makes a handy knife-sharpening gadget that clamps onto the blade to maintain the proper angle. The blade, with the gadget attached, is then simply swept across the stone.

If your knife produces a "wire edge" (you will be able to see this when you hold your knife up in the light), you will need to hone it on a strop or on a piece of heavy cardboard. Simply draw the edge backwards across the strop or cardboard on both sides of the blade until the wire edge disappears.

To touch up an edge, hold the knife and lightly run the stone over the edge of the knife at a 20-degree angle. In this case, do not bear down.

Any small pocket carborundum stone is fine for touching up. For real sharpening, a big oilstone is needed. An oilstone should be at least 8 inches in length and preferably 12, and should be firmly anchored to a bench. The stone should have both medium and fine sides. Use plenty of light machine or honing oil or some other lubricant to prevent the pores of the stone from sludging. A. G.

Russell's Arkansas oilstones are the best we have ever used. With a little experience, you will find that sharpening a knife is really quite easy.

The All-Important Ax

Axmanship is rapidly becoming a lost art among campers. Modern camp stoves and modern camping grounds are the reason for it. But we still believe that if you want to consider yourself a competent camper, you must know how to use an ax well and efficiently. Axmanship is still synonymous with woodsmanship.

A camper may not need an ax on every outing. An automobile camper in a campground will not need it at all unless firewood is not provided (as in many of the Canadian provincial parks). The backpacker may find an ax just a heavy and burdensome object. On the other hand, a canoe tripper heading down a wild river in Canada would be foolish to go without one. So would a camper heading into the wilds with a packhorse string or into a remote lake via seaplane. But even an automobile camper should carry an ax. Its extra weight means nothing to him, and he can always jam it behind the spare tire in the trunk.

An ax is a very useful tool. Its blunt end can be used to pound in tent pegs and to perform many other chores around the camp. Step one in learning to use an ax is to choose the proper one. Our recommendation for an ax for all-around outdoor use is one that is single-bitted, weighing about 3 pounds, and with a 30-inch handle. Stay away from axes that are much heavier than this because they are meant for woods workers who are used to swinging a heavy ax.

If weight is a critical factor, get a lighter ax (2¼ or 2½ pounds) and one that has a shorter handle (about 24 inches). In all cases, such an ax is better than a hatchet. It will do everything that a hatchet will do and more. A person of smaller, lighter build may find a smaller and lighter ax more manageable and more comfortable to use.

When buying an ax, do not compromise on quality just to save a few dollars. That is very poor economy. When looking at axes, sight along the blade and make sure that the handle is not warped or that the blade is not set off too much from the line of center of the handle. Make certain that the head is securely attached to the handle by being firmly wedged.

Examine the handle carefully. Be sure that the grain runs parallel to the sides. Avoid axes where the grain in the handle twists a lot. This could mean serious structural weakness. The best ax handles are made of hickory, so choose one of this wood if possible. Never buy an ax with the handle painted over its entire length because paint can hide flaws and weaknesses in the wood. Remember, an ax will easily last a lifetime if you take care of it. Your choice should reflect this. Every ax should have a leather sheath to cover the head. This is not only for safety, but to prevent nicking the cutting edge.

Keeping an ax sharp is not difficult. An ax can be coarsely sharpened with a fine file. Then switch to a coarse stone, and follow this with a medium stone. The best stone for ax sharpening is a round one. It has no sharp edges to rub through a packsack, so you can carry it with you wherever you take the ax.

As a brief safety hint, never leave an ax lying around. It can cause accidents or accidents can happen to it. In camp, keep it hung in its sheath or sink its blade into the top of a stump.

Axmanship

There is a secret to cutting with an ax and it lies in the grip. Grasp the helve (the old axmen's term for the handle) of your ax with hands close together near the butt. Now touch the blade of your ax to a tree to get the right distance. As you raise the ax over your right shoulder, slide your right hand up (if you are right-handed) about three-quarters of the way towards the ax's head. As you bring the ax down, slide your right hand down the handle until it touches your left hand. Strike the tree so that the blade cuts at about a 45-degree angle to the grain. Do not try to put excess force into the swing. If you do this, you will lose on accuracy. The fastest chopping is achieved with many swift and accurate blows, not with brute force.

To fell a tree, make your first notch near the bottom of the tree on the side on which you want the tree to drop. The side on which the tree should drop is generally chosen either because the tree is leaning in that direction or because the wind is blowing in that direction. If the tree does not have a natural lean or there is no wind blowing, you can drop the tree wherever you want.

Make your first notch about half way through the tree. Tyros generally start by making their notches too narrow, and this makes cutting difficult. A good rule of thumb is to make the notch as wide as the diameter of the tree.

Your second notch should be made 3 or 4 inches above the first one and directly opposite it. When the tree begins to fall, step away to one side of the cut, not behind it. Should the top branches of the falling tree catch on another tree, the butt may snap and fly backwards several feet. Many injuries have been caused in this way.

Now that the tree is down, the next task is to limb it. You do this by standing on the opposite side of the tree from the limbs that you want to remove. In this way, if the ax glances off the tree, it will glance away from your legs. Work from the butt to the top, chopping at the bottom side of the branches. Limbing goes faster this way, and it's easier to make the cuts flush with the trunk. The next step is to cut off the crown. On small trees, this can be done with one notch all the way through. Bigger trees may require two notches, opposite one another, each going half way.

The Useful Saw

A saw is a much better tool for cutting wood or felling trees than an ax. If you have a hungry sheepherder's stove to feed, a saw becomes a must. In the hands of the average camper, a saw will cut about three times as much wood as an ax in the same length of time.

A saw is also safer to use because, unlike an ax, it will not glance off a log and slide into the cutter's foot. In the hands of an amateur, sticks or chips do not fly from a saw as they do from an ax. And best of all, a saw can be used fairly efficiently by a novice. To use an ax efficiently requires skill and practice.

There are a number of Swede or bow saws on the market designed primarily for campers. A number of these fold so that they are no more than 6-inches wide and 2-feet long. The folding or collapsible Swede saws are generally more expensive than the one-piece. They are also not as sturdy. Their main virtue is their compactness. It is difficult for us to advise you as to which saw to get. It depends on what you need. But even a Swede saw with a one-piece bow is not a bulky item once the blade is taken from it.

Swede saws for campers come with 20, 24, 30, and 36-inch blades. The shorter lengths are best for average camp use, but a 36-inch blade will be needed if big logs are involved or if there is a lot of cutting to do such as that involved in building a wilderness log cabin.

The main thing to avoid when cutting with a saw is pinching the blade in the log. Pinching ruins the set of the teeth. Saw teeth must have a proper set in order to cut well. To avoid pinching, just make certain that the end of the log you are cutting off has room to fall free. The best way of doing this in the bush is to use a stump or another log as a sawhorse.

To keep the teeth of a saw blade sharp, do not bang them on to any metal objects, rocks, or the earth. When not in use, the saw should be hung up and not left lying around. The cutting edge of the blade should also be covered by a good sheath. Some Swede saws for campers come with sheaths of tough plastic. A chunk of garden hose cut half way through makes a serviceable sheath. It can be tied on with a couple of pieces of soft wire. In a pinch, a piece of burlap or canvas can be wrapped around the blade or tied on. When the saw is being stored away for the season, the blade should be oiled lightly to prevent rust.

Much nonsense has been written about sharpening saws. It is supposed to be a mysterious science that only a talented few can undertake. Hogwash! While it is true that sharpening a saw and setting the teeth require some experience, it is by no means difficult.

Any camper with a dull saw and a small file can touch up a saw blade, even perhaps do a creditable job of sharpening. The secret is to work slowly and to follow the cutting angles on the saw blade's teeth. If you do it carefully, there is no way that you can ruin the saw. Once you get out of the bush, you can have the saw fully sharpened by an expert.

A Word about Chain Saws

Chain saws today are seeing wider use in the hands of outdoorsmen than ever before. The main reason for this has been the development of light, easy-to-use saws with direct-drive chains designed principally for outdoorsmen and not for woods workers. The engines on these small saws generally have 2 to 3 cubic-inch displancements. Their weight, including bar and chain, is about 8 pounds.

We use a chain saw occasionally, mainly because it can cut a lot of wood in a short time, leaving time for the more enjoyable aspects of camping or fishing. This is probably why other campers and outdoorsmen also use chain saws.

The best places to use them are in areas where firewood is free for the taking. Many campers along the Alaska highway use chain saws for bucking up firewood from fallen, dry trees. Dry standing trees can be utilized as well. Certainly no living tree should ever be felled for firewood, even in a wilderness area where anyone seldom ventures. Green wood burns very poorly.

Chain saws are not difficult to use. Safety is the main consideration. Every manufacturer of chain saws encloses a booklet with the saw telling the purchaser how to operate it and how to use it safely. Always read these instructions fully.

Basically, cutting with a chain saw is no different from cutting with a Swede saw. Felling trees with a chain saw is also basically the same as felling with an ax. The notches have to be cut the same way and the tree's natural lean and direction of the wind have to be taken into account.

Chain-saw users should be considerate of other campers because it is such a noisy instrument. Restrict its use to the mid-day hours.

The Handy Shovel

No automobile camper should venture on to a forest road without a shovel in the trunk of his car. A couple of summers ago, we met a camper who learned this the hard way. As he was driving down the road, a deer jumped out into his path. He swerved to miss the deer, and his side wheels went off the road and stuck in the soft shoulder. He could not even jack the car up because he needed a shovel in order to get to the jack under the car. He tried using some sticks, but they were not good enough, and he didn't even have an ax with which to improvise a decent digging stick. He had to wait for over half a day until a car came along with a towing cable and pulled him out. With a shovel he could have dug himself out in less than half the time.

The best shovel for an automobile camper is a short spade. It is sturdy and designed for tough work. It is also short enough to fit into the trunk, even the trunk of a compact car. If a short spade is still too large, then a folding army shovel is the next best choice.

Backpackers and canoe trippers may also find a shovel handy for digging latrine ditches. This is particularly true when there is an entire group traveling together. One shovel is enough for the group and nothing bigger than an army shovel is needed. A pair of canoe trippers or backpackers may find a stone mason's trowel adequate for latrine duty. It is smaller and lighter than a spade. Kelty makes one for this purpose out of tough plastic, which is even lighter than a metal stone mason's trowel and it won't rust. A latrine ditch or hole should not be dug too deep or it will seal the human waste from bacteria which will quickly decompose it. And latrine ditches should never be dug near water.

In the old days, a shovel was needed for ditching around the tent, but tents with integral floors have largely eliminated this need. If there is a major downpour and a ditch is needed, then an army shovel will do the task. A trowel will do for ditching around a small two-man tent.

Needless to say, ditching should be kept to an absolute minimum. Also, ditches should be filled when you break camp. Remember that in most camping grounds ditching is not allowed.

Also, in the old days, a shovel was used to bury garbage. This can no longer be tolerated, even in the wilderness, or our backpacking trails would be lined with mounds of bare earth from buried garbage. If you packed it in full, you can certainly pack it out empty. Paper and such, can, of course, be burned.

Other Useful Tools

The automobile camper should always carry a good tow cable or chain with him in the trunk of his car. This may be useful not only if you have a breakdown, but also for pulling yourself or someone else out should your car get stuck. We have even used our tow cable for pulling fallen trees off forest roads.

Tire chains can also be useful if you get bogged down in snow and ice or in greasy mud. Chains give added traction almost anywhere.

An extra rope is always a good idea. You never know when you might want to lash something down or tie something up. A guy on your tent may break. Or you may want to build a fly or lean-to out of your spare ground sheet for extra shade. An extra ground sheet may also be handy.

No camper should go anywhere without a good first-aid kit. The automobile camper will find a comprehensive first-aid kit a good bet. Here we mean one of the big $25 first-aid chests, not the $3.99 discount special. The wilderness camper should carry with him a mini kit, but in some ways a first-aid kit is even more important in the wilderness. An automobile camper can always drive to get medical help, but the wilderness camper has to rely on his own resources.

Your family physician can suggest a list of items that you should stock. We have discussed this subject at some length in our book, *The Complete Outdoorsman's Handbook*.

The wilderness camper should also carry with him a survival kit. There are a number of these on the market, but many contain items of dubious survival value. Good kits are made by Eddie Bauer, Orvis, and possibly others. Any experienced outdoorsman, however, should be able to assemble a kit of his own. Remember that a different kit is required for surviving in northern Canada in the winter than for surviving in the desert country of the southwest.

Here are some of the items that the kit should contain: a small compass (spare to your cruiser compass), a small but sturdy folding knife (again a spare to your regular knife), a spare rescue blanket, a stainless-steel signaling mirror, a whistle that produces a shrill, piercing sound for signaling, 50 feet of 20-pound test monofilament fishing line, 2 dozen hooks of assorted sizes, 3 or 4 fishing lures, a 20-foot coil of snare wire, windproof and waterproof matches, a flint and steel or steel match, 2 cubes of chemical fire starter in case no dry tinder can be found, a small candle, 2 or 3 needles and a coil of strong thread for sewing torn clothes, a couple of sticks of freeze-dried meat sealed in plastic. Most of this equipment can be packed into a small leather belt pouch such as are sold by outdoorsmen's outfitters. A web canvas pouch purchased from an army surplus store is just as good and much cheaper, but of course not quite as attractive.

Besides all this equipment, we assume that the camper will have in his pocket or on his person a good quality knife, a small pocket whetstone, a waterproof container of strike-anywhere matches, and a good cruiser compass on a lanyard around his neck.

There are some good signal flares available which could also be included. But alas, all of the better flares can only be fired from a shotgun or a rifle. A hunter should include half a dozen such flares in his kit. The pencil-sized flares frequently advertised in outdoor magazines are not very good. We have tested a couple of different brands and found that we could not get them to fire above the tree line.

Every outdoorsman venturing into the wilderness should, of course, know the basics of wilderness survival—signals, edible plants, and how to trap game. These skills may save your life. They are all part of being a good outdoorsman, and that's what every camper should be.

The Life-Saving Compass

Having or not having a compass can mean the difference between being lost and finding your way back to camp. In extreme cases it can even mean the difference between life and death. No one should go anywhere in the bush, not even just to fish a lake up the mountain, without a compass. The small-town newspapers in the western states and northern Canada often carry reports of outdoorsmen who have done exactly that and gotten lost.

The compass is really just a magnetized needle, with one end always pointing to the magnetic pole of the earth. The magnetic pole, incidentally, lies 100 miles south of the true North Pole and slightly to the west of the 100-degree meridian. Despite the rather simple principle on which the compass functions, it is surprising what can be done with it.

Compasses come in many designs and in a wide range of sophistication. Compasses used for navigation and surveying are sophisticated instruments. For a camper, a compass need not be too elaborate. The needle should float in oil to dampen its swinging and the housing should have sights for taking headings. A compass with these features is called a cruiser compass because of its frequent use in timber cruising by foresters. Two good compasses in this class are the Sylva T15 and the Suunto KB14. A good compass costs from $15 to $25.

The Personal Warbag

It may seem silly to write about the personal items that should be taken along, but it is these—the toothbrush, the spare eyeglasses—that frequently get left behind. A toilet kit containing such items as toothbrush and paste, comb, nail clippers and file, soap, towel and washcloth, and mirror (preferably an unbreakable one but an automobile camper can get away with glass), razor and shaving lotion or soap is a good thing to have prepacked and ready for any trip.

Other essentials that should go into the warbag are: extra medication if your doctor has you on some sort of prescription medicines, headache tablets, and spare eyeglasses. Contact lens wearers must bring along the various liquids and lotions that go with the lenses. An extra pair of sunglasses is a must for a boat or winter camping or a desert backpacking trip.

Women may want to include various skin creams and lotions which, as Jerome puts it, makes them more slippery at night. A tube of lip balm is essential for canoe trippers, boat campers, or anyone else who will be camping where winds are prevalent.

The warbag must also contain the special interest equipment. Binoculars are a must for wildlife enthusiasts, and certainly a spotting 'scope, the kind rifle target shooters use, is worthwhile too. Other things that can be packed along in a light rucksack include a plant press for amateur botanists, a watchglass or some other powerful magnifying glass for rock hounds and phycologists, camera equipment for lens bugs, extra lenses, camera bodies, and film. Rucksacks designed for mountain climbers are excellent for camera equipment and films and, if you get the type with the ice ax straps, it can be used to carry a small tripod or monopod as well.

To all this, you may add various field guides for birds, trees, wildflowers, rocks, and minerals. Do not forget to include a voluminous paperback or two, a deck of playing cards, and even a compact set of checkers. Rainy days in camp can be boring.

It is, of course, the mode of transportation that determines what items you can take and what you must leave behind.

For winter camping or mountaineering, a down parka is a must, unless you are doing a lot of snowshoeing or ski touring, both of which generate a lot of heat.

CHAPTER 11

Garb for the Camper

Choosing clothing for camping is largely a matter of common sense. Comfort and practicality should take precedence over fashion and appearance. Aside from being comfortable, camp clothing should be rugged and sturdy. The only other dictates are those of weather and climate. You should dress with the anticipated temperatures in mind. However, don't ever forget that you may hit abnormal weather as well. This is particularly true the farther north you go or the higher up into the mountains you climb. So, as the saying goes, be prepared. If temperatures suddenly plummet, you cannot go home to get a warmer jacket.

The amount of clothing to take on a camping trip depends on the length of the trip and, of course, on the method of camping. If you are automobile camping, you have much more room and weight is no problem. On the other hand, the backpacker and the canoe tripper have to consider bulk and weight. We feel that no one should venture out, even for a weekend camping trip, without one complete change of clothing. This may actually be adequate for even a camping trip that is two weeks long. Our experience has been that campers frequently bring too much clothing with them.

Give Your Feet a Break

A camper can generally put up with many discomforts and still function and even enjoy himself but, if his feet knock out, he is finished. Have you ever tried to pack out of the mountains with a blister on the back of your heel the size of a silver dollar? We have! Even on an automobile camping trip, such a blister would ground you. It would prevent you from exploring a nature trail or hiking over a hill to find fishing in a more secluded lake.

The first requirement of good camping shoes is comfort. Be sure that your shoes are well broken in. Never go on a camping trip with only one pair of brand new shoes. A hiking trail is no place to break them in. The second is that the shoes actually give some protection to your feet. Sandals and thongs may be fine for the beach or a city park, but even the campsites of the more popular camping parks are bound to have rocks and roots protruding from the ground where it is quite easy to stub your toes. We have seen that happen more than once.

Hiking boots with lug soles and foam-padded velds have become standard footwear among backpackers.

Your selection of footwear depends largely on the type of camping you do. A canoe tripper may find that a pair of sneakers are all he needs, particularly if his portages are fairly short. Canvas boat shoes with thick crepe soles and definite arch supports are even better, but more expensive. Both types are light and dry quickly so that you can use them for wading over rock-studded shallows. They are also washable, a handy feature if you have to wade across swamps and bogs but do not like sloshing through the mud and muck in your bare feet.

If your canoe trip involves a fair amount of portaging and hiking, you may find that a pair of sturdy leather boots are needed as well. However, leather is poor for stomping through water and dries very slowly. We know that the Indians used moccasins, but that is all they had. They also used moccasins for all of their walking and horseback riding. That does not mean that moccasins are the best footwear for either pastime.

We can, however, borrow a page from the Indians and choose as light a boot or pair of shoes as is practical. The best lightweight walking shoes are Chukkas, Desert Boots, and Wallabees with thick crepe soles. If Wallabees are chosen, they should be the high-ankle type. We have worn all these shoes for months on end in terrain ranging from the savannas of Africa to

Light hunting boots, 8 inches high and made of soft leather, make excellent boots for heavy-duty camping. Some boots, such as these Dunhams, are silicone-treated for water repellancy.

the hard lava rock of the Galápagos Islands. They are comfortable enough for lounging around camp and sturdy enough for fairly strenuous hiking. They come both in men's and women's sizes.

Another suitable camping boot is a light hunting boot, the best being the so-called "bird shooter." These boots are generally made of a soft leather and are 8 inches high. Some brands are silicone-treated for water repellency. They are surprisingly light and quite comfortable. They are our choice for fall camping when we frequently combine camping with grouse hunting. For more rugged camping, Durham Dura-flex or Greb Kodiak boots are hard to beat. For loafing around the camp, we bring along moccasins with rubber soles.

For pure and simple hiking and particularly for backpacking in rough hilly terrain, we abandon our Wallabees and don a pair of hiking boots. Hiking boots are a fairly new concept in footwear on this continent, but then so is walking for fun; walking for fun with a heavy pack on your back is even newer. In Europe hiking has been a popular pastime for decades. That is where hiking boots were invented and that is where some of the best ones are still made.

There are three main types of hiking boots on the market—trail boots, scrambling boots, and climbing boots. Climbing boots are for mountain climbers. They are specialized boots and are of little concern to campers. Trail boots are fairly light, 3 to 4 pounds in weight. They have foam-padded velds and a scree guard. They are designed for trail use. Scrambling boots lie somewhere between trail boots and climbing boots. They are heavier, weighing 3½ to 4½ pounds, generally leather-lined, with a padded tongue, thicker soles and more ankle support. They are meant for trail and cross-country use. Trail boots sell for $20 to $35, while scrambling boots cost $25 to $45.

Hiking boots can be distinguished by their lug soles. The most commonly used soles are Italian-made Vibrams. The lug soles give a firm grip on all surfaces that a camper is likely to encounter, except ice or iced-over rocks. The biggest problem with lug soles is that they can cause a surprising amount of environmental damage on soft moist earth. Some of the more popular hiking trails in our national parks have been closed to hikers because of the erosion caused by lug soles. Even on mountain meadows, these soles can be damaging if too many hikers walk over the same area right after a spring thaw or heavy rains. Lug soles can cut right through grass roots.

The solution, or at least the partial solution, is to use crepe-soled shoes such as Wallabees or Desert Boots. These shoes are perfectly adequate for hiking in foothills and on the lower slopes.

Hiking boots have become almost status symbols, so much so that they have become "fashionized" by footwear manufacturers and are sold to youngsters not for hiking but as the "in" thing to wear on one's feet. Despite having lug soles and scree collars, these fashioned boots are useless on the trail. The best way a novice can avoid such boots is to stick to the better-known brands or buy his boots from a reputable outfitter. Some of the best brands on the market today are Dunham, Vasque, Danner, Pivetta, Munari, and even the J. C. Penney #6824 boot. Other outfitters such as Eddie Bauer and Eastern Mountain Sports sell their own excellent brands of hiking boots.

Buying hiking boots requires a bit more care than buying street shoes. This is not only because hiking boots represent a fair investment, but also because they must fit properly. The success of your trip may well depend upon your boots. Since hiking boots are normally worn with two pairs of socks (a light inner pair of nylon or cotton socks and a heavy pair of wool or wool-and-dacron blended socks), that is the way you should try them on in the store. But first, have the salesman measure your feet when you are wearing your two pairs of socks. Then obtain a pair of boots in the size fitting the larger of your two feet (most people's feet are not exactly equal in size).

To get a proper fit, follow these steps. Slip into the boots wearing the double pair of socks and leave the boots unlaced. Now, move your foot forward as far as possible. To make certain that it is as far forward in the boot as it will go, gently kick the toe of the boot against a wall. Then stand fully erect and have someone insert an index finger down into the boot behind your heel. If there is not enough room for an index finger in the boot, it is too small. On the other hand, if the index finger slides in with a lot of room to spare or even two fingers can be inserted, the boot is too large.

If your boots have passed this first test, move your foot back in the boot. Kick the heel in a similar manner and have someone lace up the boot fairly tightly. Now do three or four deep knee bends. You will probably feel your foot move in the boot. This movement should be about one eighth of an inch and not much more. If it is more, the boots are too large.

The final step is to have someone hold the laced boot firmly to the floor while you try to rotate your foot in the boot with a lateral motion. There should be little or no movement in the ball of your foot.

The important thing to remember, however, is that a boot must never be too long or too short or you will walk up some blisters. The width of a boot is not critical. But if your foot slides around from side to side it makes walking more difficult and the foot becomes more fatigued. If the foot fits too snugly into the boot and becomes uncomfortable as the day progresses, the foot will swell and heavy walking will be difficult.

The design and inside dimensions of boots vary from maker to maker. You may have to try several different brands and styles before you find a perfect fit.

Buying boots through the mail is not wise. However, if there are no stores in your area that handle the type of boots that you want, you have no other alternative. When ordering boots through the mail do a trace of your foot size—both feet. Step on a piece of paper with double socks and have someone trace the outline of your feet. Then mail this to the outfitter, specifying that he size the largest foot. When the boots arrive, follow the fitting procedure as outlined in the previous paragraphs. Walk around in the boots, on a carpeted floor because the lug will leave scuff marks on tile or parquetry. Do not walk with the boots outside or they may become soiled and unreturnable. If you have to return them, explain in an enclosed letter why and where the boots did not fit. It might not be a bad idea to do another tracing and perhaps mark the areas where your foot felt too tight or too loose.

Next to the Skin

Your choice of undergarments depends almost entirely on the time of year and, of course, on your personal preferences. Cotton is generally preferred by most people. It absorbs perspiration, doesn't itch, is easily washable, and is the best bet for moderate-weather camping.

For late fall and winter camping or for camping at high elevations where weather and temperatures fluctuate greatly, wool is better. It is not only warmer, but it is warm even when wet with perspiration. This cannot be said for cotton. Alas, there are many people who cannot tolerate wool next to their skin. It itches terribly. The solution is cotton next to the skin topped by wool. Don two sets of underwear—a very light one of cotton followed by a woollen one. This is excellent in cold weather but somewhat bulky.

An easier solution is underwear made of a cotton and wool blend or a cotton, wool, and polyester blend, or underwear that comes in two layers, cotton on the inside and wool on the outer side. Underwear of cotton, wool, and polyester in a blend has the advantage of being machine washable and dryable.

The fishnet type of underwear is very popular with some outdoorsmen. It works on the principle of trapped air creating an air space between the skin and the first layer of clothing. Fishnet underwear is ideal if woollen underwear is to be worn over it. Its only disadvantage crops up in backpacking, where the straps of the usual fishnet undershirts can dig into your shoulders, compressing and irritating. To overcome this, wear fishnet underwear with full-knit shoulders such as those made by Allen-A. Undershirts are versatile. They can be used as T-shirts during the noon-day heat. The colored shirts, including fishnet, even look like T-shirts.

The only other type of underwear to consider is the insulated kind. This is only suitable when extremely cold weather is anticipated. It is best for winter trips on snowmobiles. Insulated underwear is too bulky and much too warm for snowshoeing or skiing. The best use for insulated underwear, we have discovered, is as pyjamas for sleeping on winter camping trips.

Colors Can Be Important

In country where blackflies, mosquitos, and other biting insects are common, the camper should avoid dark colors—black, navy blue, and the like. Why? Because dark colors attract biting insects; blackflies and mosquitoes in particular.

We prefer soft fabrics, nothing scratchy or noisy. This is because our hobby is wildlife and wildlife photography. When we are trying to stalk a moose who is busily munching on lilypads, we do not want to warn him of our presence by having a twig brush noisily against a stiff jacket. This is why big-game hunters wear soft clothing.

We prefer the more subdued colors for much the same reasons. It makes us less conspicuous. Sure, mammals are color-blind, but it is harder for them to see slow-moving dull-colored objects than it is to see slow-moving colored objects. This is why professional hunters in Africa, many of whom are extremely fine naturalists, always wear khakis and neutral colors.

Of Shirts and Sweaters

Layering is the right way to dress for camping, or any other outdoor activity. Not only are two lighter shirts warmer than one heavy one but, if the combination gets too warm, you can always take one off. The day may begin cool and fresh, but by lunch-time temperatures may have risen 20 or more degrees and you may have worked up a fair amount of body heat laboring up steep and long portage trails.

It is really immaterial what combination of outer garments one uses. For example, a turtleneck sweater followed by a medium-weight shirt are excellent, particularly for cooler weather. The turtleneck is better than a scarf. Two shirts are also good, the inner one of flannel or light wool and the outer one heavy wool. The best outer shirt is made of pure wool. Get one that is tightly woven. Outer sweaters should be made of wool, particularly in the fall or when in the mountains. Sweaters of raw wool, wool that has not been blanched, are best. This wool retains natural lanolin and is surprisingly water repellent. Sweaters of raw wool may be rough in appearance, but camping trips are neither fashion shows nor cocktail parties.

In recent years, down sweaters and vests have become very popular. They have several advantages over wool. They are warmer for their weight and they compress into smaller bundles, which makes them particularly handy on backpack trips into the mountains or on canoe trips into the north country. Down sweaters are ideal for ski touring. During the day, the skier sweats up a storm; but at night while he is cooking supper, it can become pretty chilly. A down sweater in a packsack is worth its weight in gold.

Pants and Slacks

Modern pants and slacks are frequently designed more with fashion in mind than with comfort. They are too tight around the hips, buttocks, and crotch. Make sure your pants do not constrict any of your movements but are loose and comfortable.

Weather dictates the type of material and the type of trousers that should be worn. Wool is best in late fall or winter. This is where women campers run into problems. Wool slacks for women, particularly rough work-type slacks, are almost nonexistent. Women's libbers arise! However, by shopping carefully, a woman can find suitable woollen pants. The biggest problem is wide flares and wide cuffs. Flares let in the cold and the bugs. They also catch on things and flap about in the wind. Wide cuffs pick up almost every seed, twig, and piece of debris that is likely to be encountered.

Women who want to wear woollen slacks may have to alter them. A slight flare, incidentally, is fine if you are wearing boots above the ankle. The flare should be about the same as on the trousers of Mexican cowboys, so that it slips over the boot tops quite easily.

Men have it a lot easier. Good woollen pants can be found in many stores that cater to men who work outdoors. The best places to find woollen pants are the lumbering towns of the northwest, the upper Great Lakes states, New England, and northern Canada. Some of the outdoorsmen's outfitters like L. L. Bean or Eddie Bauer also sell woollen pants. Army-issue wool pants are one of the last great surplus buys. With a few alterations, such as inserting a nylon zipper and belt loops, they make good cold-weather camping pants. Eddie Bauer also sells trousers of dacron and cotton blends, lined with woollen melton cloth. They are available in both men's and women's sizes.

For summer camping, denim is still one of the best materials available. Avoid the western-cut jeans. In most cases, these are too tight and uncomfortable. Work jeans are better and cheaper. However, as we mentioned earlier, dark blue is a bad color during fly season. It attracts more bugs than the lighter colors. We find the so-called safari pants hard to beat. They have a comfortable cut and were designed with hiking in mind. They are khaki, a good color for the bush. At least one of the outdoorsmen's outfitters is now marketing special hiking pants, for both men and women, made of a cotton and dacron blend, which appear to be excellent. When buying pants for summer, again avoid flares and wide cuffs.

Shorts are very useful for warm days, except in bug country. Again, shorts should be fairly loose-fitting so that they do not bind and chafe around the thighs. Shorts are a popular item with European hikers, and European-style hiking shorts are making an appearance here. We have some, and we like them very much. They are sturdy and are reinforced in the critical wear areas. However, no one should go camping dressed solely in shorts. Always have long pants along in case of inclement weather.

The only other trousers that we have not mentioned are knickers. At one time, knickers were the proper golfing attire. Today they are staging a mild comeback. This is probably due to the recent ski-touring craze. There is no doubt that knickers make fine camping pants, particularly for backpacking. With long wool socks right up to the knees, wool knickers are as fine for fall camping as they are for ski touring.

The Neglected Socks

Socks are frequently the forgotten items of outdoor apparel. Somehow campers feel that if it does not show, it doesn't matter. But socks are a very important piece of wearing apparel. They are part of the footwear package.

On an autombile camping trip, any sort of cotton socks are fine. Chances are that you will not be wearing anything more substantial on your feet than a moccasin loafer, so no other socks are needed. However, for any sort of hiking, you must treat your feet better. In summer, we recommend one pair of soft, fluffy socks of a wool and synthetic blend. Such socks absorb perspiration and give lots of comfort by acting as cushions. In cold weather, we return to the layering principle and use a pair of cotton socks followed by a pair of woollen ones. Those of pure wool are warmer than the blends, but they require special washing and drying care and are more expensive.

Silk socks are even better than cotton for cold weather. They have many insulating air cells that trap air and heat. They are preferable to cotton, but also much more expensive. Silk inner socks and woollen outer socks are the best combination for very cold weather.

Down jackets are the best bet for the backpacker. They are only a quarter of the weight of a wool jacket of the same size.

Socks must be kept clean at all times. Dirty, matted socks offer less insulation than clean ones. They also invite foot troubles. Many experienced backpackers and hikers change their inner socks at mid-day during a hike. They also wash their socks daily, generally in the evenings so that they can dry overnight. An extra tube of biodegradable soap occupies less space that a couple of pairs of extra socks.

Parkas and Jackets

The season of the year, latitude, and altitude will determine the final selection of your outer garments. You will not need anything heavier than a cotton shirt for a camping trip on the beach on the Gulf Coast of Texas in midsummer, but, on the other hand, a chilly spell can settle in on the coast of Maine, even in midsummer. Anyone planning a summer camping trip in the north temperate latitudes from New England across central Canada and right over to Washington, should include a windbreaker in his dufflebag. The mornings and evenings can be chilly. Fishing on a windswept lake can be a chilly or even numbing pastime if a cold front has moved in from the north.

Something a bit heavier than a light windbreaker will be needed for backpacking trips into the mountains of Alaska and Canada. A combination wool sweater and windbreaker is good at the height of summer. A couple of wool shirts and a windbreaker are also fine. But towards the end of August, the air will have a hint of fall and the temperatures may dive to freezing at night, with snow flurries coming as early as the beginning of September. The camper should be ready for this and have a more substantial jacket with him.

Undoubtedly down garments are best for the backpacker. The reasons for this are the same as the reasons for using down sleeping bags. The thickness or loft of the down garments depends entirely on the season of the year. For late summer or early fall, the so-called down sweater is a good choice. It rolls up into a compact bundle in a backpack, and it is there if needed.

There is a large selection of down clothing on the market, and Frostline even has kits for the do-it-yourselfer.

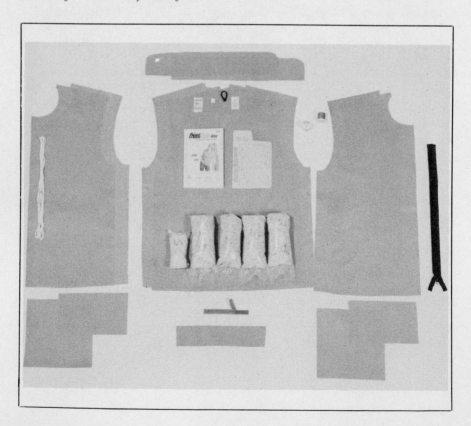

As fall approaches, the camper's clothing must reflect changes in temperature. The automobile camper can make do with a wool jacket or with jackets where wool provides the basic insulation—many hunting jackets are good.

For winter camping in sub-freezing temperatures, down is again the best bet for the snowshoer. Many of the better outfitters offer down parkas that are good for sub-zero temperatures. These are much too warm while on the trail. In comparison to down jackets, they are fairly bulky. Our preference is for medium down jackets that have a comfort range from sub-zero to 60 degrees Fahrenheit. If the mercury dips much below this, we rely on the garments under the jacket to keep us warm.

Despite its many virtues, down is not perfect. If it gets wet, its insulating qualities go down the drain. Wet down mats, and matted down is useless. This is one area where wool is superior. The other problem with down is its cost. Unless you will be doing a fair amount of cold-weather camping, and backpacking in particular, a down jacket may not be worth the investment.

The snowmobile camper will find that a snowmobile suit is an excellent camping garment as long as he does not try to do too much walking in it. Snowmobile suits were designed for the sedentary. They are too bulky and too hot for snowshoeing or any of the other more active winter sports. If you plan to use a snowmobile to get you into the back country with your tent and your other gear, and if from there you plan to hike around on showshoes or cross-country skis, you will have to bring clothing that is suitable for these activities.

Miscellaneous Wear

The hat is a very important item of clothing. If you are camping in hot, open country—the beach or the desert—a sun hat of some sort is a must. The best hat for such occasions is one with a wide enough brim to shade your eyes.

A baseball cap is favored by many. The long-billed Gulf Coast fishing hat is also excellent. Cowboy hats are suitable as well. Our favorite, however, is the helmet-shaped fishing hat of cotton and polyester twill such as those sold by L. L. Bean and Orvis. The shape of this hat is ideal for shedding rain and providing shade.

For fall and winter, a toque is a good choice. Any hat with ear flaps, however, is good. Our personal choice is a tam-o-shanter of wool. It is practical, warm, and has a jaunty flare. In cold weather it can be pulled right over the ears. For extremely cold weather, balaclavas and fur-lined arctic hats are the best choices.

For cold-weather camping, gloves are an essential piece of clothing. The important thing about gloves is that they be flexible and actually allow you to grasp things with ease. Gloves of wool or wool and nylon blends may be suitable. The so-called shooting gloves of soft deerskin or pigskin are good if the weather is not too cold. In cold weather, a pair of silk gloves inside a

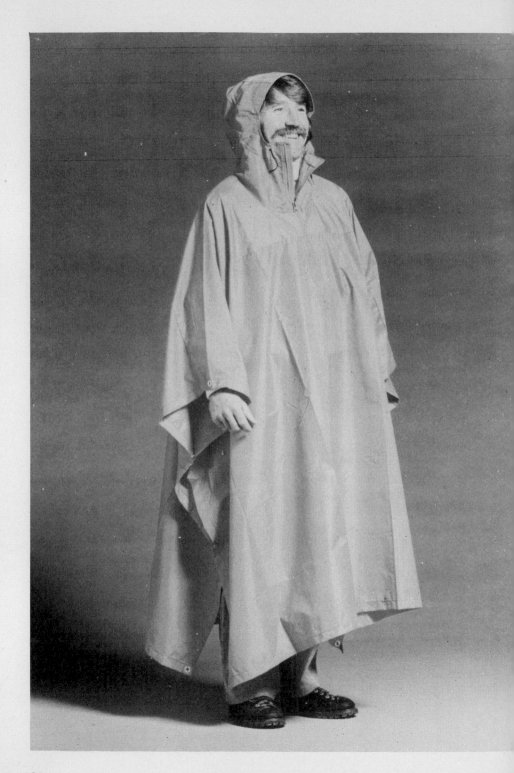

pair of leather roping gloves is an excellent combination. In extremely cold temperatures, down-insulated mittens along with a pair of light gloves may be needed.

A large bandana is very useful. On hot days in the desert, it can be used as a sweat band around the forehead. If you are hiking through bug country, you can soak it with insect repellent and tie it loosely around your neck. It keeps out the bugs and is more pleasant than smearing bug dope on your face. In an emergency, a bandana can serve as a washcloth, a towel, a potholder, a handkerchief, and even a bandage.

The only other item of clothing that we commonly take along on camping trips is swim wear.

Raingear

Raingear is a nuisance. The only bigger nuisance on a camping trip is the rain itself. An automobile camper can get along very well without any raingear. If it starts to rain, he can take cover in his tent, his camping trailer, or his car. The canoe tripper and backpacker do not have that advantage. It seems that rain always strikes just as one is paddling across a wide lake or hiking up a steep trail.

The main problem with raingear is that it is hot in warm weather and hot even in cool weather if you are working up a sweat by hiking up a portage trail. There have been times during brief summer storms when we have found it more convenient to get wet from the rain rather than our own perspiration.

The old poncho is the most versatile piece of raingear. Essentially it is nothing more than a small tent with a slit at the top for the head or a hood. The features to look for in a poncho are size and quality. A poncho should be big enough to cover the backpack. For the backpacker, the best poncho is of light, coated nylon. Such a poncho will weigh less than a pound, but it won't be cheap—$10 or more for the better quality ones.

The automobile camper will find a poncho of rubberized cotton adequate. This is the old army standby. It is just as waterproof as the nylon poncho, probably even more so, and is much cheaper—generally about $5. Its disadvantage is its weight, about three pounds. Avoid the cheap plastic ponchos for treks into the bush. Their lives are very short.

The problem with a poncho is that it flops around in the wind, catches on brush along the trail, and it won't keep you dry much below the knees. One of the virtues of a poncho is that it can double up as a ground sheet, a very useful feature if your backpacking tent has no floor.

Another useful piece of raingear is the long rain parka. The rain parka is more manageable than the poncho, but you cannot put a backpack under it.

A poncho is a versatile piece of rainwear for the camper, but it flops around in the wind and will not keep you dry below the knees.

99

It is therefore of much more value to the fisherman, and the fisherman is the man for whom it was designed. It is also handy for working around the camp during the rain.

The two-piece rainsuits are the best for keeping dry. The problem with most rainsuits is that they are too flimsy and fragile. They just will not stand up to the rigors of outdoor activity in the bush. The best rainsuits are of rubber, such as those used by fishermen on commercial fishing boats. But these are too heavy and too bulky for the camper.

The only really suitable rainsuit for the outdoorsman is the Scottish Bulkflex of knitted nylon coated with polyurethane. It is tough and durable. The knitting process creates capillaries which let the rainsuit breathe and allow some heat to escape. This rainsuit is sold by Orvis and by Bob Hinman Outfitters. The price runs about $80.

Two-piece rainsuits are best for keeping dry. Do not skimp on quality. The cheap ones are flimsy and never last.

Planning is the key to any successful camping trip. To avoid the crowds, plan your trip for June or after the middle of September when the campgrounds are nearly empty. If fishing is your bag, you must plan your trip for when the fishing is best. For trout, it generally means spring or fall; while walleyes and northern pike bite all summer long.

CHAPTER 12

Planning Makes the Difference

Planning a camping trip can be a lot of fun. It builds up a feeling of anticipation; and it brings back memories, both good and bad, of other camping trips. Even bad memories are useful—they remind you of what not to do.

Planning is one of the keys to a successful trip—to any successful trip. A weekend campout can be spur-of-the-moment but, if you are planning to be out much longer, you should plan. This is particularly true for the peak summer season when campgrounds are filled to the rafters.

The old cliché "it's never too early" comes close to being the truth when planning for a camping trip, especially a wilderness camping trip. For example, many of the horseback outfitters in the western states and in western Canada are frequently booked a year ahead. The same is true for canoeing outfitters in such popular areas as the Quetico wilderness. Even the simple act of getting maps by mail can take a fair amount of time. So begin planning early.

What Type of Trip

The first step is to determine what type of camping trip you want to go on. An automobile camping trip to the western parks? A backpacking trip in the Appalachia? A wilderness fly-in trip to northern Quebec? A boat-camping trip on one of the Great Lakes? Where do you want to go? Your interests, age, state of health, the number of people in your party and their ages, and even the type of equipment you own all have a bearing. If you are 60 and have a bad heart, a backpacking trip is out. If you have six kids, a fly-in trip to the Quebec wilderness may also be out. Chartering enough aircraft space to fly in gear, groceries, and people would be very expensive. You may not have a suitable boat, nor wish to rent one for a boat-camping trip. Your final decision on the type of trip may be arrived at partially by the process of elimination.

On the other hand, you can decide on a particular trip solely because of special interests. Fishing is a frequent one. Wildlife photography, bird watching, and rock hounding may be others. Perhaps you want to make a tour of old ghost towns in the west. The possibilities are endless.

The Nitty Gritty

The high price of gasoline may also be an important consideration in your decision of where to go. The old chestnut about distant pastures always looking greener describes a very common human trait. But now is a good time to consider areas closer to home. You will be amazed at how much there is to do and see within 200 miles of home. If you draw a circle on a map using 200 miles as the radius, you will come up with 125,600 square miles. That is a lot of territory to explore.

When to go can also be difficult to decide. If you have school-aged kids, the only time you can leave is when school is out. But in July and August the highway traffic is heavy and campgrounds are crowded. In many of the national parks, getting a campsite on the campgrounds can be a serious problem unless you have a reservation. The wilderness camper can still escape, even in summer, but the automobile camper must be prepared for crowds and facilities that are filled to capacity. For summer automobile camping, planning is not merely helpful, it is a must. An automobile camper who likes peace and quiet will find that spring and fall are much better. Crowds after the Labor Day weekend are almost non-existent. September is a beautiful time to camp. The heat of summer is past, and the cold and rains of fall have yet to come.

Weather is an important consideration in planning a camping trip. If you do not like heat and humidity, don't go to Florida in midsummer. Similarly, if you don't like dry searing heat, avoid the desert country of the southwest during summer. Spring and fall are more hospitable times in both areas. Winter is a good time for a Florida camping trip.

If fishing is your main interest, then you must correspond your trip to peak fishing periods. Trout fishing is best in spring or fall. Bass fishing in the south and southwest tends to be slow in the hot weather of July and August. On the other hand, northern pike and walleye bite throughout the summer in northern Canada. Saltwater fishing is generally best in the summer months, but the Gulf Coast and the waters around the Florida Keys offer fishing the year around.

Information, Please

One of the critical things that campers frequently neglect is to research their destination. The more you know about the area you intend to visit, the better you are able to plan what to do and see. For example, friends of ours, both archeology and anthropology enthusiasts, spent a couple of weeks at a campground that was only about 20 miles from an important archeological site of an ancient Indian village. They knew nothing about the site until we asked them, on their return, what they thought of the "dig." Had they obtained a tourist booklet published by the local chamber of commerce beforehand, they would have learned of the site.

Local chambers of commerce or tourist associations in the major resort areas are an excellent source of information. They will gladly send free travel brochures on request or, stop at information offices and visitors' bureaus.

There are a number of good sources of camping information. Rand McNally, Woodall's, and Sunset publish up-to-date directories of campgrounds. These are available at newsstands or bookstores and can be a tremendous asset when planning an automobile camping trip. They not only list campgrounds along the major highways, but also those in out-of-the-way places.

State travel or tourist bureaus are also good sources of camping, travel, and outdoor recreation information. Most states and Canadian provinces publish booklets describing their park systems. Some even publish maps showing the locations of the parks. They also have literature describing each park in detail, including camping facilities, hiking trails, and canoe routes. Ontario, for example, has a brochure on every one of its hundred-odd provincial parks, describing the park and including the opportunities for fishing, wildlife, areas of historical interest in or near the park, plus other pertinent information. Many states and provinces publish directories of private campgrounds. They also have publications on canoe routes and hiking trails. And, of course, they all publish a considerable amount of information for the fisherman and hunter.

The U.S. federal government has much useful information for campers intending to camp on or near federal land. The Bureau of Reclamation operates campsites on some of the lands in the western states. Information, including maps, is available free of charge from the Information Office, Bureau of Reclamation, Washington, D.C. 20240.

Regional offices of the National Parks Service, listed in the appendix, are good sources of information on camping in the national parks. Maps are available showing backpacking trails and canoe routes. Regional offices of the National Wildlife Refuge, also listed in the appendix, are good sources of information for wildlife enthusiasts and hunters.

The Office of Information, Department of the Interior, Washington, D.C. 20240, has many useful publications. Photographers may find a copy of "Outstanding Photographic Opportunities on National Wildlife Refuges" very useful. Campers who like to travel into the byways, the little-known areas of the national parks, will find a copy of "Lesser Known Areas of the National Park System" very interesting.

Whenever you are writing for information, try to be specific. State the type of camping you want to do. If you are interested in a canoe trip, there is no point in being sent a packet of information on campgrounds for automobile campers.

Children like to help with the letter writing. It is a good experience for them and it gives them a role in planning the trip, but be sure to cast the odd supervisory eye over their efforts.

Anyone contemplating a wilderness trip should have good topographical maps of the area. These are available from the Map Information Office, U.S. Geological Survey, Washington, D.C. 20242 (for maps east of the Mississippi River); or the Map Information Office, U.S. Geological Survey, Federal Center, Denver, Colorado (for maps west of the Mississippi). Maps of Canada can be obtained from the Map Distribution Office, Department of Mines and Technical Surveys, Ottawa, Canada. Canoe trippers will find the American Canoe Association, Incorporated, 400 Eastern Street, New Haven, Connecticut 06513, a useful source of information.

Check Your Gear

As the departure date for your camping trip draws near, the final plans and preparations must be made. Your tent and other gear should be checked to ensure that they are in good repair. If you have a new tent, be sure to pitch it in your back yard first. This is a good idea even for a tent that you have been using for many seasons. It serves as a check to ensure that none of the poles or pegs are missing. A new tent should be broken in by spraying with water.

If you have a new recreational vehicle, you should take it on the road for a short shakedown run, for a weekend trip, before attempting a long trip with it. Every rec vehicle should be serviced at the start of each camping season. This is also the best time to give it a thorough cleaning and test the stove, heater, and refrigerator.

If any servicing must be done on your car or recreational vehicle, do not leave it to the last minute. If you have a foreign car and are traveling with it in out-of-the-way places, you might consider stocking a few emergency parts, the type of thing that may go suddenly. Getting parts for your car may be no problem at home, but in a small town in Montana it could be another story. If you have a foreign car, be sure to have a list of all dealers in North America. You may never need the list, but if you do it will be invaluable.

A week or two before departure date, draw up a list of gear and clothing that will be needed for the trip. This way you have time to think about your choices and to make sure that this is what you want and need. Also, you minimize your chances of leaving any pertinent equipment behind. Invariably, when a camper packs too quickly, something is forgotten.

CHAPTER 13

Camping with Wheels

Automobile and recreational vehicle campers outnumber all the others—the backpackers, the canoe trippers, the horseback packers—several times over. The proliferation of camping parks is good evidence of this.

Automobile camping trips are comfortable, convenient, and simple ways to camp. Automobile camping requires none of the rigors of backpacking. It needs no highly honed outdoor skills. Even a city dweller whose outdoor experience is limited to walking from his office to the subway and from the subway to his apartment can go on an automobile or a rec-vehicle camping trip, make a success of it, and enjoy himself.

How to Pack

The best type of luggage for an automobile camping trip is the duffle bag. Duffle bags are better than suitcases, because they fit into corners and crevices much better. The disadvantage of duffle bags is that they are soft. If you intend to visit cities along the way where you may need to dress a little better, then a hard suitcase is a must so that your good clothes will remain relatively uncrushed.

Every camper should have his own duffle bag. That goes for kids as well. Ideally, everyone should be responsible for his own clothing and personal items. This does not always work out, but a stab should be made at it anyway. A good thing about duffle bags is that they are relatively inexpensive and come in a variety of sizes. The only good duffle bags are those with the zipper across the top and two carrying handles, one on either side of the zipper. The navy-type dunnage bags are simply too inconvenient.

As you pack, check the items against your list. Once you have all the gear and clothing packed, it is a good idea to go through a practice run in packing the car. You will learn how things fit in best. For example, while packing the car on one of our earliest camping trips, we discovered that we had too much gear. Since the trip was to be a long and complex one, we felt we needed everything we were taking. However, since it was a Friday evening, we still had time to purchase a roof luggage rack before the stores closed at 9 o'clock. We were able to depart at daybreak on Saturday as planned.

If you have enthusiastic fishermen in your group, put their tackle near the top. Many anglers like to try their luck in lakes and streams along the way. If the tackle is on top, it makes things much easier. If you are taking rifles or shotguns along, make sure that they are fully encased. It is illegal to carry uncased firearms into national parks, into many state or provincial parks, and into wildlife refuges. Handguns can present special problems if you are crossing state lines. Find out beforehand what regulations are in force. Generally a visitor may take an enclosed and unloaded shotgun or rifle across any state boundary, but this does not apply to handguns. Forget about taking handguns into Canada or Mexico. Actually, even taking rifles or shotguns into Mexico involves a staggering amount of red tape. If you intend to do some hunting, it's easier to rent one there from your guide.

A Word about Luggage Racks

For an extended camping trip, particularly in a compact car, a luggage rack is often needed. Although the roof rack can be used to carry just about any item, we find it particularly useful for the tent, cooking kit, and such tools as axes, saws, folding shovels and, if necessary, rolled-up sleeping bags. If sleeping bags are to ride on top, they must be packed in plastic bags and then in a canvas duffle bag. The duffle bag is then put into a large garbage bag made of heavy plastic meant for industrial use.

The best luggage racks are those that are permanently attached to the car. Ordinary sedans normally do not have this option, but station wagons and the various hatchbacks do. Otherwise any sturdy luggage rack will do. Be sure that the hooks that grip the automobile's rain gutters are covered with vinyl or plastic. If they are not, cover them with a bit of electric tape, so as not to scratch the car. Be sure that the suction cups are fairly deep so that they grip the roof firmly. The carton in which a luggage rack comes generally has the rack's load capacity printed on it. Stick to it.

Lash everything down tight. When you are traveling at 50 or 60 miles an hour, that's a gale force wind tugging at your gear. If your luggage rack is the removable kind it must be cinched down very tightly. It is actually not a bad idea to cover all of the gear with a tarp or an extra ground sheet, even if you are not anticipating rain. Then lash everything down. A luggage rack cover may also be a good idea, particularly if you are going to be carrying suitcases and other items that should not get wet.

Luggage rack covers are easier to put on than tarps with a lot of lashings and knots, but they are generally restricted to specific loads. A tarp and rope are much more versatile. If you want a luggage-rack cover and cannot get one to fit your rack, any awning maker or canvas dealer can make one to suit your needs.

We do not have a luggage rack cover. We feel that unless one does a lot of traveling with goods on the roof of the car, the investment is not warranted. While on the subject of luggage racks, there are on the market

The automobile camper needs no highly honed outdoor skills to make a successful trip and enjoy himself. Nor does he need the rigor or stamina of the backpacker or canoe tripper.

what could be called luggage trunks, made of fiberglass or high impact plastic. These are streamlined for shedding rain and for wind resistance. They offer more protection than any canvas, but their design makes them useful only for specific loads. They are too short for most cottage tents, for example.

Whenever you are traveling with luggage on the roof, after a few miles of fast driving stop and check your load to make certain that the lashing is still tight. Every time you stop for gas or other breaks, get into the habit of checking the load. We always carry an extra coil of nylon rope and a couple of elastic shock cords in case our luggage needs more lashing.

In many cases, trailering a canoe or even a light boat is easier than carrying it on top of the car. Two canoes can easily be pulled on one trailer. However, there are a good many boat and canoe racks available on the market. One can even get a canoe rack made of styrofoam blocks for cars without rain gutters. Lashing a boat or canoe down is easy. A rope fore and aft, or on bow and stern, and then down to the bumper is usually all that is needed.

On the Road

When traveling to an unknown destination, the passenger in the front seat should be the navigator. The driver should focus all of his attention on his driving. On turnpikes and expressways, navigating is easy, but in the back country, it's a bit different. Here a driver cannot do a good job of both navigating through the maze of back-country roads and secondary highways and driving.

The navigator can keep track of the direction on road maps and watch out for road signs. If at all possible, the driving chore should be shared by a number of people. They can change places every two hours or at every fill-up.

If the trip is taking you through hilly or mountainous terrain or through the hot deserts of the southwest, the driver should glance at his gauges, the heat gauge in particular, much more often because in these areas cars overheat more readily than on flat stretches.

Extra oil and extra water should be carried in any isolated country. So should an extra fan belt. Keep the gas tank full, even if it means filling up when it is only down to half. Also, the driver should pay extra attention to the car itself. He may be able to hear or spot things before anything serious happens. If you have been on the road for several days, periodically check your tire pressure.

Traveling speed should not be dictated solely by the legal speed limit. A car that's heavily loaded or one that's pulling a camping trailer will be harder to stop at the same speed as one that is nearly empty. Do not try to bite off more distance than you can comfortably cover in a day. We feel that 500 miles is a very long day's trip, even on good, straight highways. A distance of 300 miles is plenty for the curving and hilly roads of New England. Some people seem to enjoy chalking up miles on their trip. It is almost like a race to them. That is no way to enjoy an automobile camping trip. Visiting local sights and attractions adds immeasurably to any trip. After all, seeing and experiencing are two of the reasons for traveling.

Kids can become bored during long car trips (actually so do adults, but we seem to be able to bear it a little better), so it is not a bad idea to devise some car games. Older children can help with the navigation. Coloring books may help to amuse smaller children. Actually, coloring books and story books are a must for rainy days in camp anyway. Having children keep a count of wildlife passed on the roads can also help. A friend of ours, a well-known outdoor writer, once had his kids count dead wildlife along the highway. This was tabulated on a per-mile basis. The wildlife carnage so shocked him that he obtained other information and wrote a major magazine article about it. Obey all deer-crossing signs. The number of automobile accidents involving deer and other big-game animals is staggering. Big game on highways are a serious hazard, but we will have more to say about this in a later chapter.

Stop fairly early in the afternoon. Campsites in most parks are still given out on a first-come, first-served basis. By getting there early, you get a better choice. We have also seen more than one camper turned away because of lack of space. If you pitch your camp early, you still have time for some pleasurable activities. Wildlife watching is best in the early evening. That is when many mammals feed. Fishing is also often at its best at this time.

If you ever have a breakdown on the road, get the disabled car away from the pavement as quickly as possible. A raised hood and a white cloth tied to the door handle are the international distress signals. If your car is disabled, we feel it is better to stay with it unless you know that help is nearby. If there are several adults in the party, one can go for help. We have found that in isolated areas people stop to help much more readily than on busy highways. You should always help a motorist in distress. In our world of violence and robberies, it may not always be wise to stop except where there is a family involved. But you can always phone the police from the next gas station. Someday you may need help yourself.

If your car has broken down at night, be sure to put up a warning light or a distress flare. Every motorist should carry these with him at all times.

On the Campground

As we said earlier, in the chapter on planning a camping trip, campgrounds in many of the national, state, and provincial parks tend to be crowded in the summer months. This means that courtesy and consideration are two essential commodities. Alas, they are not by any means common. Most of us go camping to escape from radios and television. If you want to bring your transistor radio or TV along, that is your privilege, but its volume should be turned down, particularly at night. The same applies to other noises. If you want to have a sing-song, that's fine, but first find a secluded spot for it.

Always park your car off the road by pulling it into the campsite. If you are camping in the desert country of the southwest, keep at least one of the windows a bit open. In forest country, do not park your car under or near any dead trees or near trees with dead limbs. These may be knocked over in a windstorm. On the other hand, a shady place to park your car is always nice.

Finally, always respect the camping park's rules.

Canoe camping is enjoying an unprecedented boom. The wilderness rivers of northern Canada that have not been traveled since the fur-trading brigades of the last century are now being paddled by modern voyageurs.

CHAPTER 14

Waterway Camping

Waterways—lakes and rivers—have been man's paths of travel since time immemorial. They still are. Many of our waterways, however, are used today only for recreational travel. The wild rivers of Canada, New England, and the West are good examples. The days of the fur-trading brigades are long over. Today's voyageurs are pleasure seekers. The log drives are also over and even the many canals built to transport coal, iron, and other goods and wares in flat-bottomed barges are used today largely by pleasure boaters.

Almost any kind of waterway, as long as it is deep and quiet enough to float a craft, may be used by a canoe or boat camper. Canoe camping is enjoying an unparalleled boom, whereas boat camping has gone largely undiscovered.

On Canoes and Canoeing

The modern canoe is a highly versatile craft. It can be paddled, poled, and even rowed. It can be sailed or propelled by a motor. It has a reputation as a tricky craft requiring the hand of an expert, but this is true only in rapids frothed with white water or on lakes when a storm has beaten the water into whitecaps. There are places and times when a child of eight can easily and safely paddle his own canoe.

Which Canoe?

Tyros find choosing a canoe a perplexing matter. It is not only that the novice lacks experience, but that he has not developed any likes or dislikes. Choosing a canoe involves selecting the design, length, and construction material. A brief chapter such as this one can give only the highlights of how to choose a canoe and indeed of canoeing techniques.

For canoe tripping, the traditional double-ender is the only choice. The ends should not be too high or they will catch too much wind. The floor should be fairly flat for stability and for good load-carrying capacity. The canoe should have some keel to stiffen the hull and save wear and tear on the bottom. The keel will also aid in keeping a straight course. A keel-less canoe is for white water and rapids. It is much more maneuverable and responds much more quickly to paddle strokes than a canoe with a keel. However, white water is not for tyros.

A canoe should be 16-feet long. Such a canoe will carry two people and enough gear for a 2-week trip. If longer trips are to be made or if you are canoeing with a child, a 17-foot canoe is better. Stay away from the 14 and 15-foot canoes. They are too small for two people and their gear on any extended canoeing trip.

The three basic materials for canoe construction are fabric and wood, fiberglass, and aluminum. There are other materials used, but they are much less common. Each of these materials has its advantages and disadvantages. Aluminum is sturdy and light but it is noisy and hot. Fiberglass is cooler, smoother, and heavier than aluminum. It is tough and, if a puncture does occur, easy to repair. Both aluminum and fiberglass canoes are maintenance-free. Fabric and wood is the traditional material and hence appeals to purists. It is light, fairly sturdy, unsinkable, and cool in summer, but it requires maintenance. It is also expensive.

Canoe paddles should reach from about the paddler's nose to the ground. For canoe tripping, the blade should not be wider than 4½ to 5 inches. For quiet, deep water, spruce paddles are the best. They are light. For this reason they are also ideal for women and kids. For shallows and rapids, hardwood paddles are better. They are tough and strong. Ash, hard maple, and yellow birch are good woods for paddles.

Canoemanship

Learning to paddle a canoe is not difficult. There are many types of strokes. The choice of which to use depends on what the canoeist wants to achieve. A canoeist who knows the four or five major strokes is well prepared for any kind of canoeing.

In paddling a canoe, both the sternman and bowman sit. On a choppy lake or in white water, however, they kneel to bring the center of gravity of the craft lower. Kneeling for long periods of time is a cramping and tiring business.

The most-used strokes are the bow stroke, the quarter-sweep, the bow draw, the pitch stroke, the fish-hook stroke, and the Indian stroke. Any book on canoeing will describe how to do these in detail. But, in each case, as in casting with a flyrod, a demonstration is better than all the written instruction in books. Experience is really the best teacher.

Loading, launching, and landing a canoe are also techniques in themselves. When loading a canoe, it is best to carry everything to the water's edge and then load the canoe in a balanced way. Aluminum and fiberglass canoes are easier to load than wood and fabric because they can be run up onto the beach. A fabric and wood canoe must be floated parallel to the shore. The sternman gets in first and the bowman kicks off. Avoid scraping your canoe on the bottom. This applies particularly to fabric and wood canoes. As you kick off, the bowman backs the canoe out and swings it around into the direction you want to head. Landing a canoe is much like launching one, with the sequence reversed. It is the bowman's responsibility to watch for rocks.

If choppy or white water is anticipated, it is wise to lash or snap-swivel all your gear to the thwarts. Then, if the canoe capsizes, you will not lose any of it. Your spare paddles should always be on top so that you can get to them quickly if the one you are using snaps on a boulder in white water.

The canoe should be launched at right angles to the shore if at all possible. The bowman may have to jump out suddenly if a boulder looms. Approach all unknown landing sites with caution.

Canoe Tripping

When one thinks of a canoe trip, wilderness comes into mind. A wilderness canoe trip may well be the highlight of canoe camping, but it is not the only one.

Canoe tripping is generally associated with New England, the Great Lakes states, and Canada, but the waterways of the south offer unique and interesting canoe routes. The famed Okefenokee Swamp of Georgia is a prime example. The swamp is laced with canoe routes from 2 to 5 days in length. In places where no dry ground to make a camp exists, wooden platforms for tenting have been built. The Everglades of Florida are another good canoe tripping possibility, but no one should venture there without a guide.

There are many rivers that do not flow through wilderness that can be canoed. And when it comes to making camp at night, you will be surprised how easy it is to get permission to pitch your tent on a riverbank farm, as long as you promise not to leave anything behind. These rivers are ideal places for the tyro canoe camper where he can perfect his technique and toughen his muscles.

The same applies to some of the bigger inland lakes, including the big reservoirs of the southwest and midwest. You can paddle along the shore, making a circular route. Many of these inland lakes have campgrounds, so finding a place to camp is no problem. On these camping trips, you do not have to carry too much in the way of provisions because you can buy things more or less as you need them.

Old canals from the days of steam tugs, or even earlier when barges were pulled by beasts of burden, are interesting places to canoe. More and more people are doing it. Many of these canals are now publicly owned. And even the waterfronts of big cities offer unusual camping facilities. Canoe trippers have paddled around New York City from the Hudson River Parkway to Jamaica Bay, a 5-day and 120-mile canoe trip.

The equipment for any canoe trip should be light and durable. The lighter the load, the easier it is to portage. Backpacking equipment that includes lightweight tents and rucksacks or backpacks is ideal. Usually you can be a bit more generous with your equipment on a canoe camping trip than on a backpacking trip. This generosity depends on the length of your portages and their number. On our canoe trips, we generally find that we need to make two trips across portages—one trip with the canoe and a load of gear, and the second with two loads of gear. We do not load our bags of gear too heavily.

You should always bring along a spare paddle. On a wilderness canoe trip, a pair of spare paddles is a must. Equipping yourself for a wilderness canoe trip is no different than for any other wilderness camping trip. Because wilderness canoeing is generally done in forested country, an ax is indispensable. Even if you are not a fisherman, bring some simple tackle along with you. The fishing is frequently very good and the fish are a welcome addition to the menu. The key element is self-reliance.

Boat Camping

Camping with a boat has not received as much attention as canoe tripping or other types of camping. This surprises us. Boats offer an easy and comfortable form of transportation. Boat camping offers many of the advantages of automobile camping—the ability to take large, roomy tents and lots of gear—but at the same time a boat enables the camper to reach more secluded spots. We have found that boats and canoes are an ideal way to watch marsh and water birds as well as other wildlife. And, of course, they enable us to fish areas that are inaccessible to the land-based angler.

River tripping is very popular in the west and mid-south. The wild rivers of the west and of Canada's northwest can be floated down for an exciting trip. The waters are rough and turbulent. Too rough for a boat. Big rubber rafts are used. These are outfitter trips for campers who want to try something different. The outfitter supplies everything except the sleeping bag and personal items.

Many of the Ozark streams in Missouri and the limestone streams of Kentucky and Arkansas are ideal for boat camping. Indeed, this is where boat camping was developed, mainly by fishermen after smallmouth bass. There are guides in these regions who take out campers on 3 or 4-day float trips in comfortable john boats. These rivers are clear running and beautiful.

Boat camping does not lend itself to wilderness travel as well as canoe camping. Getting gasoline in wilderness areas is one problem. Thus boat camping is best done on big lakes and rivers close to urban areas. Many, if not all, of the rivers flowing through the southern half of this continent can be boat camped.

The Great Lakes offer unique boat-camping potential. Lakes Ontario, Erie, and Huron have many camping parks along their shores. Lake Superior, on the other hand, offers some prime wilderness areas along its coast that are easy to reach by boat. One of the best spots is the 10,000 island area of Georgian Bay on the Canadian side of Lake Huron. This area is easy to reach and offers plenty of marinas for refueling. The scenery is beautiful and there is no shortage of places to camp. Many of the islands and even parts of the mainland are public land. Even some of the uninhabited private islands are open to camping if you burn nothing but driftwood. There are also several fine provincial parks and one national park in this area.

The large impoundments of the south and midwest offer excellent boat-camping opportunities. The big reservoirs on the Colorado River, such as Lakes Powell, Mead, and Willow Beach are good areas. Oklahoma's Lake Eufaula, for example, has two state parks and 17 campgrounds. Turtle Creek reservoir in Kansas has 11 camping parks on its shores. The reservoir complex on the Missouri River in South Dakota forming Lakes Lewis and Clark, Francis Case, Sharpe, and Oahe is another. In Texas there are many impoundments, such as Toledo Bend, Sam Rayburn, and Amistad on the Rio Grande. Lake Amistad is ideal for someone who likes to camp on undeveloped campsites.

The south has its big reservoirs, such as the TVA lakes. Kentucky's 101-mile-long Lake Cumberland is a fine bet for boat camping. Bull Shoals and Table Rock in Missouri are two others. An entire book could be written about the camping and fishing possibilities in the reservoir lakes, which number into the hundreds.

A good thing about boat camping is that no highly specialized equipment is needed. The same gear that you use for automobile camping is fine. A 16-foot boat can carry as much as a car, and, if you intend to be continuously on the move, pitching camp in a different spot each night, an easily erected tent is a necessity.

No one should venture out on a boat-camping trip without essential parts for the motor and some tools. A pair of oars and a paddle are musts. These should be on the boat at all times. Other essential items are: extra life preservers, an extra anchor, extra rope, and extra gas tanks. A small trolling motor, to act as an auxiliary motor, is a good idea if you are heading out into less-traveled waters.

Boat campers should bring raingear and windproof jackets in case the weather turns cold. Sunglasses, suntan lotion, and lip balm are other necessary items, as are containers of drinking water.

Charts and navigational maps are necessary if you have a big boat. Cruise slowly in unfamiliar waters. Have a good quality transistor radio and extra batteries on hand so that you can be warned about bad weather well in advance. At the first hint of a storm, hit a sheltered bay or a marina.

One last tip about any canoe or boat camping trip into the wilderness or into less developed areas—always tell someone, for example a forest ranger or a marine operator at your jumping-off point, when you will be back. If you are late, they can instigate a search.

CHAPTER 15

With Your Camp on Your Back

The popularity of backpacking is a new phenomenon. It is a product of today's society, mostly of the young. In a way, like the bicycle, the backpack and hiking boots are backlashes against the over-mechanization of our world. They are symbols of the freedom of wild and unspoiled hills.

The popularity of backpacking, like the popularity of canoe tripping, is one of those gentle breezes that periodically refreshes the outdoor recreation scene. Sales of backpacks and hiking boots far outrun off-the-road motor bikes. We hope that this will always be so. Mountain trails should always be the domain of muscle power and not mechanized horsepower.

Just as canoe tripping is largely associated with the east, backpacking is associated with the west. The mountain trails of the west are, in many ways, ideal backpacking terrain. Barring an exception or two, like the myriads of hiking trails in the Appalachia, there is nothing in the east that can compare with the mountain country of the west.

Backpacking is generally considered suitable for adults or adolescents. Yet any child of six or seven can walk well enough to go on a backpacking trip, even carrying a few pounds on his back. The secret lies in not making the trip too long. A night or two out is about right, and you should knock off early in the day. An exhausted child will not enjoy himself. The pace of the party must be geared to that of the child. Infants can be taken on backpacking trips as well. There is no shortage of backpack baby carriers on the market.

Between two and five are awkward years for backpacking with children. Kids are then too heavy to carry and too young to be able to walk very far.

How to Walk

To become an expert at it—or even just a competent walker—one must learn how to walk properly. To accomplish this, no special instructions are needed. No manuals full of technical advice have to be read. To learn how to walk, you go out and walk.

The first step in becoming a good walker is to be in good shape. Almost any kind of exercise—jogging, calisthenics, handball, bicyling—is good for

Backpacking is enjoying an unparalleled boom. The backpack and hiking boots have become symbols of rebellion against our over-mechanized society. They conjure up images of mountain vistas and unspoiled hills.

this. But the hiking trails themselves provide the best conditioning of all. You begin with short trips on easy paths in fairly level terrain and, as your leg muscles tighten and your heart and lungs discover what exercise is all about, you take on longer and steeper trails.

Walking down a busy city sidewalk does not prepare anyone for walking on a trail. Stopping for traffic lights, and weaving and dodging among other pedestrians is no way to develop rhythm. A smooth rhythmical stride is essential for becoming a good walker. The only place to develop such a stride is where you can walk uninterruptedly so that your mind is free to wander, free to slip into daydreams. Once this happens, your bones, ligaments, and muscles take over and propel you in the way they were designed, in the way that God and nature intended.

The right pace depends on many things. The type of terrain, altitude, and quality of trail all have a bearing. You cannot walk as quickly uphill as you can in level areas. If the trail is rocky and uneven or has many blowdowns across it, you will have to pay attention to where you put your feet. This will slow you down. Mountain sickness strikes some people as low as 7000 feet. You cannot walk very fast or very far if you are feeling nauseous. Mountain sickness is caused by lack of oxygen, so the only cure is to pump more oxygen into your lungs.

Other factors that influence the pace are the physical condition of the walker, the load he is carrying, and even his age. A man with a 60-pound pack on his back does not walk in as sprightly a manner as a man with only his lunch. Similarly, a man who has kept in shape during the winter months ski touring will be able to walk faster and longer than a man who has been hibernating.

Age can be an important factor when setting the pace. A child of eight may not be able to walk faster than a mile every 45 minutes, while a hiker in the prime of youth can make a mile every 15 minutes without even exerting himself.

It is foolish to set a pace so fast that soon your legs feel as if they were made of lead, your lungs ache, and your heart sounds like a kettledrum. You are punishing yourself. Hiking and backpacking should not be ordeals. Hiking is supposed to be, at least in part, a communion between yourself and nature. If the hawk soaring in the sky or the yellow-bellied marmot whistling from a nearby slope does not take your mind off your legs and lungs, you are walking too fast.

How far to walk also depends on the individual. For many people, six hours on the trail a day are enough, while others do twice that. The same criteria that establish pace also affect distance. Your personal interests must also be taken into consideration. We know backpackers who like to linger over wildflowers and mosses, and others who will abandon all thoughts of going any further if they can add a new bird to their check list. We like to stop and photograph or to try our luck at trout fishing at every inviting lake or alpine stream. To each his own. The backpacker's world is free, big, and easy.

Sage Advice

For uphill travel, you must develop what experienced hikers call the "rest step." At first this will require conscious effort on your part, but as you get into the swing of it, your unconscious will take over. The rest step goes like this: advance one foot, pause momentarily to give the forward leg a rest with the knee bent and no weight on it, and then advance the other foot and pause momentarily. With each pause, you take a deep breath, filling your lungs to capacity.

The second secret of hiking and backpacking is to rest periodically. A five-minute rest every 30 or 40 minutes does wonders for the constitution. And, if you are gaining elevation or nearing the end of the day, a rest every 15 or 20 minutes is even better. Rest recharges the batteries and the will to go on.

The frequency of your rests and their length should be in proportion to all the other circumstances that affect hiking and backpacking. A man with a heavy pack on his back will need to rest more often than a man carrying nothing. The faster the pace, the more frequent the rests. Kids and older hikers need rests more frequently, as do out-of-shape hikers.

Avoid mad dashes. These always lead to exhaustion. A mad dash followed by exhaustion can have a debilitating effect on your system. For older hikers, it can be like committing suicide. And to boot, it does not get the hiker into shape any faster. Experienced hikers keep a steady pace.

The Staffs of Life

The backpacker will soon find that ultimately his welfare will rest on four things—food, water, salt, and sleep. The last is the least problem. Even if you are a chronic insomniac, we guarantee that 10 hours of hiking in fresh mountain air will make you sleep like you haven't slept since childhood. A backpacker needs plenty of rest to function well.

He also needs a steady source of fuel for his boiler. Healthy exercise creates healthy appetities. Extreme weariness tends to depress it. We have, on an occasion or two, been so weary that the thought of food did not enter our minds, but after resting for an hour or two we were ravenous.

The backpacker, like the canoe tripper, works harder than any other type of camper. He burns up more calories. His diet must reflect this. We have never heard of anyone gaining weight on a backpacking trip, but a loss of weight is common and welcome for many.

Aside from being light, foods for backpacking must be highly nutritious and rich in calories. Meats, and carbohydrates in the form of sugars and starches are best. Ideally, the backpacker's lunch should be an all-day affair. You should have a bite of food every couple of hours or so. In this way the stomach will never become overloaded. Chocolate, raisins, other dried fruits and nuts, all mixed in a concoction known as "gorp," are ideal to munch on. The occasional sip of fruit juice is welcome as well. A shot of sugar revitalizes the system very quickly. However, do not take an excess of sweets suddenly. In some people a complex physiological reaction can take place in which the blood sugar is decreased. Nausea and light-headedness will result.

Backpacking frequently produces a fair amount of sweating, particularly as one labors up a steep slope. Sweating causes not only a loss of water, but loss of salt as well. A slight salt deficiency results in a sort of general weakness, while in more severe cases it can produce nausea, headaches, and muscle cramps in the legs. A salt tablet every few hours will replace any salt that is lost. The salt tablet should be taken with water and, even better, with food. In many cases, salt tablets are not necessary. More frequent use of salt at mealtime is often enough. And the excess use of salt can also create other hazards. Consulting a physician on this is a wise precaution.

Your intake of water depends on how hard you are sweating, but it is not unusual for a backpacker to lose up to two quarts of water a day and, in the hot arid regions of the southwest, it may be twice that much. So drink plenty of water. Debilitation by dehydration is not as uncommon as one might think. We sample every mountain spring and brook on our travels, and keep our canteens full. Do not gulp too much cold water at one time because it shocks the system. Drink often and in moderation.

The Load on Your Back

Just as a child must learn how to walk before it learns to run, a potential backpacker must also learn to become a hiker. Only after a few day-long hikes with a light rucksack on the back should backpacking be attempted. And even then, our advice is to begin in easy stages with light loads. Try a few overnight hikes first. One-night campouts won't require much food and equipment. Many books on backpacking flatly state that a human can carry a pack weighing one third of his or her weight. This is true, but how far and for how long? And which human?

The capacity to carry loads varies tremendously from one person to the next. There are a host of other variables as well. Experience is one. An expert backpacker can generally comfortably carry a bigger load than a tyro. A 180-pound man suffering from a bad back which, incidentally, is common among millions of people, may find even a 25-pound load unpleasant. A backpacker who is overweight already has an extra load to carry.

Distance and pace also enter into it. A 60-pound load may be acceptable if you plan to cover only five or six miles a day or if all of the walking is on good trails over relatively flat terrain.

The best advice we can give you is to go slowly and test your own back. Then proceed from there. We have found that for reasonable comfort the weight of a backpack should not exceed 25 percent of the backpacker's weight. This means that the average man can carry enough food, clothing, and gear for a week to 10-day trip. Anything over 10 days is a long backpacking trip. In our opinion, it is beyond most people's enjoyment.

Packs for Your Back

It is almost impossible to go on a day-long hike without carrying something, even if it's only a lunch. For a backpacking foray of 10 days, the amount of equipment needed is considerable. About the only place a man can go on a walking-camping trip and not have to carry much is in Africa. We once spent a week camping in the northern sector of Zambia's wildlife-rich Luangwa Valley National Park. We were there to photograph the big beasts of Africa—lion, rhino and, particularly, elephant. We carried only our photographic equipment, which was considerable, while our string of five porters carried the rest of our gear. Each man carried about 30 pounds plus his own "katundu" with a bag of mealy meal and an ax.

The governments of Africa encourage employment of Africans by tourists on safari. This is a way of sharing the tangible benefits of wildlife among all concerned. It provides revenue. To us, having porters was an unheard-of luxury. The porters even insisted that they take along a galvanized metal tub for our bath.

However, for camping on foot on this continent, we all have to carry our own gear. But how? Essentially there are three types of packs—the fanny or belt pack, the rucksack, and the backpack. There is also a packframe and even a vestige of the old days—a back basket.

The fanny pack is essentially a small pack that is buckled around one's middle. The pack rides on the back just above the buttocks. The fanny pack was designed for small loads—2 or 3 pounds. It is ideal for carrying a lunch, perhaps a small can of fruit juice, a couple of rolls of film, and perhaps an extra camera lens if it is not too heavy. The fanny pack becomes uncomfortable to carry if it's overloaded. It was designed for day hikes, ski touring, or similar types of trips. Many of the leading manufacturers of backpacking equipment—Kelty, Camp Trails, Wenzel—make fanny packs.

The rucksack, in its modern version, is essentially a European development. Rucksacks come in various sizes from fairly small ones that hold just enough gear for a day trip to big ones that approach backpacks in size. European hikers prefer rucksacks because they frequently sleep in hostels and hence do not carry tents.

For a novice hiker, a rucksack is easy to cope with. It rides lower on the back than a backpack, so the hiker's center of gravity is lower. This makes walking easier. The rucksack is also much handier than a backpack in the bush because it rides lower and doesn't catch on branches. It is the only pack for ski touring because of its low center of gravity.

The bigger rucksacks are perfectly good packs for overnight trips. They are not as comfortable on a long haul as a backpack and their load capacity is less, but for an overnight campout they are excellent. Even the small rucksack can carry much more equipment than a fanny pack. We find rucksacks ideal for carrying extra cameras, lenses, and a good supply of film on our wildlife photography expeditions.

Rucksacks generally come with two or three pockets. They are made of canvas or synthetic fiber. Most of the better ones are made of ripstop nylon or nylon and cotton blends. Certainly nylon rucksacks are lighter and more water repellent than those of canvas. The big rucksacks have aluminum ribs in the back which can be bent in the shape of the packer's back. Such rucksacks are the best bet for carrying heavy, hard objects that have a tendency to jab the back.

The better-quality rucksacks are reinforced in the key wearing areas. They are double-stitched. The shoulder straps are padded, and they have a waist belt. The bottom of the rucksack is lined with some durable material such as heavy canvas or even leather. The snaps and buckles are all of good quality. Some rucksacks are especially designed for mountain climbers. They have loops and carriers for ice axes and other mountaineering paraphernalia. Again, the leading manufacturers of backpacks also make rucksacks. Good rucksacks are also imported from Europe. Frostline even has a kit for the do-it-yourselfer.

Modern backpacks are essentially a North American development. Their predecessor was the old wooden packframe to which bags were lashed. Today, there are scores of backpacks on the market, some of which (generally the low-priced ones) are of such poor design that "torture rack" is a more appropriate name for them.

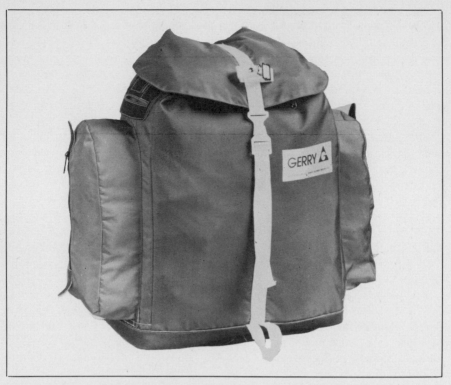

The modern rucksack is a European development. It is ideal for ski touring and travel in forests. But it does not have the load capacity of the backpack.

Backpacks are characterized by an aluminum or magnesium frame contoured to fit the body. They come in many sizes for children, women, and men of different heights. It is imperative that the frame of a backpack fit correctly, or it will not be comfortable. The best way for a tyro to buy a pack-frame is from a good outfitter with an experienced sales staff who can insure that the frame fits. Packframes, incidentally, come in three-quarter and full sizes. The three-quarter lengths are meant for short trips.

We recommend that you always buy a frame and a bag made by the same maker. This insures that the bag is designed for the frame. However, it is possible to mount one maker's bag on to another's frame. The better frames have nylon mesh back panels that help to distribute the load evenly and keep the bag away from the packer's back.

The bags themselves are made of a nylon fabric. Their capacity varies from 1500 to 3500 cubic inches of gear. Generally they have several pockets and straps or lashings for extra gear. The zippers are covered by weather guards on better quality bags. The very best have nylon zippers. Colors vary from blaze orange to forest green.

The backpack is a relatively new development. It is the best way to carry a heavy load into the wilderness.

The packframes can be fastened together by pins, eutectic weld, heliarc weld, bolted, or Lexan couplings. The last three are the strongest and best. Pins are used only on cheap frames. They are flimsy, so stay away from them. Once a frame breaks, it is difficult to repair except in the case of those with Lexan couplings. Good quality packframes have padded shoulder straps and a waist belt.

There are also heavy-duty packframes such as Camp Trail's Freighter. They have a loading platform on the bottom of the frame. They are meant for carrying heavy and irregular loads. A good quality, full-length frame sells for $35 to $45. A bag will run $60 to $80. It is difficult to get a good quality full-length backpack for much under $100. A good quality three-quarter length backpack will sell for $50 and up.

We recommend that any prospective backpacker stick to well-known brands such as Kelty, Gerry, Jan Sport, Camp Trails, Alpine Design, Sierra Designs, Mountain Master, Trailwise, REI, and Browning. Also, buy from a well-known outfitter. He will not stock junk. But remember, most manufacturers offer several lines from economy to deluxe.

The backpacker must carry all of his gear on his back. This means that everything must be light and small.

Child carriers are specialty packs designed for carrying children on backpacking trips. The biggest maker of these is Gerry, with three different models. For very young infants, there is the Gerry Pleatseat, a sort of cotton rucksack. For toddlers there is the Gerry Kiddy Seat and the Gerry Kiddy Pack. The Kiddy Pack is designed for children of up to 35 pounds. It also has a storage area for baby-type gear.

In the Gerry carriers, the child rides facing forward. This places the mother's hair and ears within the child's reach. Camp Trails also makes a child carrier called a Tote-a-Tot, in which the child faces backwards. This is fine, but some children get lonely if their mother is the last hiker on the trail. With the Himalayan Piggy Pack, the child can be carried either way. The price of these aluminum-framed child carriers ranges from $12 to $20.

Other Gear for the Trail

A backpacking trip is frequently a wilderness trip, so the backpacker should be equipped for wilderness travel. The chapter on wilderness camping discusses some of the items you will need. A good map and compass are musts. A good knife is another. Tents, sleeping bags, clothing, boots, cook kits, and other paraphernalia have been covered in the previous chapters. So what else does a backpacker need? Well, some people find a walking staff handy. In the rarely traveled forest wilderness areas, you can still cut your own at the beginning of every trip. But a walking staff of green wood is fairly heavy. Take it home if you can and leave it to dry out. It will be lighter next year. Or, you can purchase a walking staff or even a good sturdy walking stick.

A canteen is a must for most backpacking trips. Get one that is light— aluminum is the best. It should hold at least half a quart of liquid. Your food should be stored in plastic bags. The Gerry Company also makes handy tubes of plastic for jams, peanut butter, and the like, to be used instead of jars. These are a very good idea. When you want a peanut butter and jam sandwich, all you have to do is squeeze some out. Undoubtedly you will also want a container for stove fuel. The best and lightest are bottles of spun aluminum. They are durable and designed for backpacking.

The backpacker will also need a mess kit, a survival kit, a snake-bite kit if he is going into snake country, a first-aid kit, waterproof and windproof matches or ordinary wooden matches in a waterproof case, and a flashlight. Aside from these items, no other specialized gear is needed for backpacking.

CHAPTER 16

Introduction to Bike Camping

The bicycle is enjoying an unprecedented boom. The bike boom lies mostly in the hands of young people who have discovered that the car is not the only way to travel. But among this young crowd, there is a sprinkling of gray and even bald heads. Bicyling has come full circle.

The bicycle is about 100 years old. For the first 25 years of its life, it was essentially a toy for wealthy men. You had to be well-off to own one. A bike in the 1870's and 1880's cost $100 to $300, or about $800 to $2400 in today's dollars. After the turn of the century, however, wealthy men got new toys—automobiles—and the first bike boom was over. From there until the 1960's and 1970's, in North America, the bicycle was a kid's toy.

Bicycle campouts and hikes are not new. They began about the time the first bicyclist got tired of pedaling around the block. Bicycle camping was a popular sport in the 1880's. And even today's bike hikers, who have crossed the continent, have not done anything new. The first bicyclist to cross this continent did so in 1884.

The All-Important Bike

The bicycle, naturally enough, is the most essential piece of equipment for the bike camper. Any bicycle will do, but the best bet is a lightweight 10-speed bike equipped for derailleur shift and 10-gear ratios—5 gears in front and 2 in the rear. Such a bike can be used by everyone, from beginner to expert.

The front of such a bike should be made of superior quality tubing such as Columbus or Reynolds 531. The tubing must be light, but at the same time it should be strong and sturdy. Remember that it is the frame that holds the machine together.

Bicycling is enjoying great popularity, and with it has come a surge of interest in bicycle camping. But this is not a new sport. Outdoor magazines in the 1880's were full of stories about bicycle camping.

The bike can have either tubular or clincher tires. Tubular tires offer a more resilient ride and easier pedaling, but they are much more puncture-prone and are harder to repair. If you will be doing much traveling on gravel roads and even on forest trails, get the heavier clinchers. These are not as lively to ride on, but are more serviceable, and getting replacements is easier. When on the trail in warm weather, check your tire pressure regularly. It does not take long for the air inside to get warm and create high pressures. Burst tires are not uncommon, and tires are not all that easy to change on 10-speed bikes.

Brakes should be checked every time you push off. Lubricate the metal working parts periodically, but never the pads, because these work on the basis of friction. Oiled pads will not cause much friction.

Handlebars depend on the bike. With a 10-speed bike, you really should have racing-style handlebars. These are designed for most efficient bicycling. They allow you to ride low, resisting wind, and they place your body in such a position that it uses muscles other than those in the legs. Racing-style handlebars are harder to get accustomed to than the touring-type. However, once you are used to them, you will prefer them.

Saddles, again, are a matter of what you get used to. Beginners generally feel more comfortable with mattress saddles that are spring-loaded and padded. But expert bike hikers prefer narrow, leather racing saddles. Like the racing-style handlebars, one must get used to racing saddles.

The only other piece of equipment that the serious bike hiker should have on his machine are toe clips. Toe clips are a must for longer trips. Using them can mean gaining up to one-third more energy. Toe clips are U-shaped strips of thin aluminum attached to the front of rat-trap pedals. It is essential that the ball of your foot, not the instep, rest in the center of the pedal and do the pushing.

Remember to keep your bike clean and shiny. Pay particular attention to the chain. A dirty, oil-clogged chain not only looks unattractive but also detracts from the machine's operation. The best way to clean a chain is with kerosene, but if you do not want to take it off, a light oiling and rubbing with a rag will help.

Until now we have portrayed the ideal machine. As we said earlier, most of us begin with a bike that we have had in the garage for years or have borrowed. So should you. There is no point in investing in a new machine for bicycle camping until you find out whether this sport really appeals to you.

Gearing Up

The bicycle camper, of course, needs a camping outfit. His carrying capacity is limited, much like the backpacker's. So the same gear that the backpacker finds handy is ideal for the bike camper—the light tent, the down sleeping bag, the poly pad, the light cookwear and mess kit, the light stove and bottle of fuel, flashlight, matches, and all of the other small but important pieces of paraphernalia. The bike camper is spared from taking much food along. Since he stays on roads, he can generally find a store where he can buy provisions on a daily basis.

However, the bike camper does need some special gear to service his bike. A tube repair kit is one, a bicycle repair kit is another. A spare tire, a few spokes, pliers, a nail puller, an odometer, a spoke wrench, friction tape, bike lubricant, an air pump and, of course, a bicycle lock should all be in his kit. He will, of course, also need a first-aid kit as well as all his personal items. Even insect repellent may be needed.

Like every camper, the bicycle camper must dress for the weather. Clothing must be loose. This is particularly true of trousers. You cannot pedal well in tight pants. In warm weather, shorts are excellent. But one pair of long trousers should be taken along, as should a warm sweater, a windproof shell, a hat for rain or sun, and a poncho or light rainsuit. No bicycle camper should venture out on to the road without a complete change of clothing. More than that is not necessary. You can always buy more if the need arises. After all, you are not going off into the wilderness.

The serious bicyclist should have bicycling shoes. Bicycling shoes are characterized by flat and heel-less soles of very hard leather to withstand the wear and tear of rat-trap pedals. They are generally made of black leather with many holes perforating the sides and top. Good bicycling shoes are expensive. If you cannot afford them, buy any good shoes with hard soles. If you will be wearing biking shoes on the road, you will need another pair of shoes for loafing in camp.

Riding gloves are another item of specialized clothing. These are similar to golf gloves, except that the fingertips from the knuckle down are bare. The leather palms are padded where the hand grips the handlebar.

The best and the most comfortable way for a bike camper to carry his gear and clothing is in bicycle paniers or saddlebags. There are three types of bicycle bags. The best are paniers, fitted to a metal rack that is bolted on to the rear wheel fork. The bags ride on both sides of the rear wheel. Then there is a handlebar bag and a small bag that fits behind the saddle.

The saddlebags should be lightweight, sturdy, and waterproof. The seams must be especially strong. They should be relatively easy to pack and unpack. Good bicycle paniers are made by Bellweather and Gerry. The handlebar bag is a controversial item. Many bicyclists won't have one. Certainly, a bag on the handlebars does not help steering. However, we think that its disadvantages are outweighed by its advantages. However, you can't use a big bag or it will be too bulky and heavy when loaded. A bulky handlebar bag will prevent you from seeing the wheel, and one that is too heavy will be a handicap in steering. The best handlebar bag, in our opinion, is the French Solonge bag. The fourth bag, riding directly behind the saddle, is essentially a bag for tools and tire-repair kits.

It is essential that two paniers be loaded with the same weight in each; they must be balanced. The way to load them is to fill one first and to weigh it. Then

The best way for a bicycle camper to carry his gear is in paniers. The best type are those that sit on the sides and over the rear wheel fork.

---

fill the other to the same weight. The paniers should carry all of your heavy camping gear and clothes. The handlebar bag should be reserved for lighter items—personal toiletries, food for the road, maps, first-aid kit.

The only other item that should be strapped on to a bike is a canteen or water bottle. Some bike hikers also carry one of the new bicycle transistor radios. We do not. It's nice to get away once in a while from the kind of news that makes news today. If we want a weather report, we can always ask at a gas station or general store.

Before Hitting the Road

Before you hit the open road, you should map out your route. A road map is an indispensable item. There are a number of ways to plan a route, a circular route being by far the most common. The length of a route depends

132

primarily on your bicycling experience and on the time you have for the trip. Even your physical condition should enter into this. You should not plan a 200-mile tour as your first trip of the season, unless you have been exercising your legs all winter.

An increasing number of cyclists are also planning one-direction routes and then taking a public carrier—bus, train, or plane back home. Most airlines will accept a dismantled bicycle as one piece of luggage. Many cyclists are also using an automobile as a means of reaching distant points and then cycling to points of interest so that they can see the countryside more thoroughly. Bikes can be carried on a roof or on a trunk rack as easily as a canoe can.

Another type of panier fits over the handlebars. All bicycle paniers should be light, sturdy, and waterproof.

The best maps to get for bicycle camping are official state and provincial highway maps. These are kept up to date as far as new highway construction is concerned. These state and provincial maps can be obtained free of charge by writing to the tourist departments in question, or the highway or transport departments. Road maps given away by gas stations can also be used, but frequently these are out of date. Inaccuracies also seem to be more frequent.

One of the easiest ways to plan a route is to have an automobile association do it for you. This service is provided free of charge for members. If you are not an automobile association member, perhaps one of your friends or relatives is. That person could request a route plan for you.

One problem with automobile association routes is that they are planned for cars and not bicycles. Hills, for example, do not mean much to a car driver, but they are important to a biker. Routes planned for auto drivers also generally encompass expressways, many of which prohibit bicyclists. For example, if you wanted to drive from Detroit to Montreal, the most direct way is on Ontario Highway 401, the MacDonald-Cartier Freeway. Byclists are not allowed on this 4-lane expressway. Therefore if you are using the services of an automobile club, check their routing carefully.

The best way to plan a bike route is to do it yourself. You can then note such things as scenic highways. The scenery will be interesting, but such roads are generally in hilly country so you must decide between scenery and easy biking. By planning the trip yourself, you can avoid truck routes, busy streets in cities, and areas near ski resorts because these nearly always denote hills. State and provincial maps have state and provincial parks marked on them. This will let you know where to camp. They also mark points of interest and historical sites which can add immeasurably to any bike trip. The list of information that a good road map provides is amazing. All you have to do is learn how to use it.

The same applies to city maps. Here, however, avoid the heavy traffic areas if you can. Some cities have maps with bicycle routes marked on them.

Before hitting the road, become physically fit. Before going on a long bike trip, you should ride for an hour each day. Begin by riding 5 miles per hour, adding a mile or so every second day until you have reached 10 miles per hour. Then, on weekends, ride 20 miles in 2 hours.

On the Road

The speed at which you travel depends on the condition of the road (gravel or asphalt), the terrain, the load you are carrying and, of course, your physical condition. If you have followed the daily regime of bicycling that we prescribed, you should be in pretty good shape. Also, take it a little easier and slower during the first few days of your trip. When you see how you are standing up to the strain and you feel the power returning to your legs, you can speed up.

134

Work out a comfortable cadence—the number of revolutions you pedal per minute. The cadence is up to you. It is important, however, that you maintain this cadence, regardless of what gear you are in. This is one of the most important reasons for gears on a bike. By keeping to a good cadence, you develop a smooth rhythm which is a good, economical use of energy.

The number of revolutions per minute that you should aim for is not totally immaterial. Cadence has a direct bearing on your speed. A bicyclist in good shape should be able to do 70 to 80 revolutions per minute, hour after hour.

When and how to shift gears is frequently a baffling business for the beginner. However, it is quite easy to learn. The best way to learn is on the road as you pick up affinity for your bike. Just shift smoothly and easily. Pedal with an easy cadence, slowly pulling back on the gear lever. With a bit of practice, you will not have any trouble. The one thing to remember with derailleur gears is not to pedal backwards when changing gears, so that you do not accidentally disengage the chain.

You must remember not to ride in a gear that drags you down. If your legs are straining, you are in the wrong gear, providing of course your legs are in good shape. If you are going up hill, the wrong gear will hit you like a lead shoe. When the bike feels as though it is a part of you, then you have mastered the wonderful art of bicycling.

Regard automobiles as your worst enemy. Ride defensively and be alert. Some car drivers will not give you any right of way at all. Some will even deliberately crowd you out. In cities, stay away from main streets with heavy traffic. Try to time your schedule so that you do not hit cities during rush hours, and watch out for parked cars pulling out suddenly, car doors being opened and, of course, pedestrians. We have found that car drivers are generally inconsiderate of the cyclist.

We also recommend that you confine your travel to daylight hours. Night travel is always more hazardous, even if your bike is equipped with good lights, reflectors, and the new fluorescent spokes and tires. We also recommend that you not bicycle in the rain. Again, you are harder to see through rain-splashed windshields. You do not have the control and braking power that you need on wet pavement, and there is really no point in getting soaked. If rain catches you on the road, pull out your poncho and try to wait it out. Try to get under a bridge or head into a restaurant. You can even seek shelter under a big leafy tree, providing there is no lightning.

Wind can be a biker's friend or enemy, depending on whether it is blowing into his face or his back. Even a moderate wind of 12 to 15 miles an hour can aid or hinder a cyclist's progress. Do not try to buck strong winds. It is better to hole up somewhere, rest, save your strength, and hit the road at dawn the next day. You will make faster progress and expend less energy in that way. But there are times when a cyclist has no choice but to plug in and pedal away in the face of a wind.

Bicyclists should beware of stinging, gale-force winds. These can sweep around and knock a cyclist off his bike without warning. Be particularly careful on mountain passes or where roads edge around cliffs. Even a moderate wind can blow strongly here.

The only other things a bicyclist has to fear are dogs and hoodlums. A lone male biker is probably most vulnerable to hoodlums. Punks will intimidate a woman less often. There is no glory in harassing a woman. But both male and female bikers can be subjected to obscenities. Our advice is to ignore them. Ignore any threats as well. Remember that discretion is the better part of valor. The main thing is not to panic. Most hoodlums do not want to actually fight, but to prove how brave and tough they think they are. If the worst comes to the worst, scream and shout for help. Do not hesitate to get the biggest tool out of your bag or to use it.

This is another reason for not riding at night. Hoodlums are less prone to start trouble in daylight when people can see their crimes. This is also one reason for planning your city routes very carefully. There are neighborhoods where a cyclist is not safe. Do not cycle alone. A pair of bikers is better, and a group of four or six is better still. Despite having painted a picture of fear and gloom, do not let this stop you from bike camping. The danger is really quite minimal and much less so in the country where most bike campers will be heading. We recently read an account of a woman who bicycled across the United States and never once suffered any sort of hassle.

Dogs also represent a problem to hikers. A dog that would not even think of chasing a car will sometimes take off after a bike. Farm dogs in particular, seem to enjoy chasing bicyclists, probably because they do not see many. However, few dogs are vicious, although when they're chasing you they may all seem that way. A technique that has worked for us is to stop and shout angrily at the dog—"Now you fool you've caught me, what are you going to do with me?" Most dogs will stop, lower their tails, and skulk away. The main thing is not to show any fear.

In country where you have a good chance to outride a dog, particularly a small dog, do not hesitate to do so. During cycling's early history, wheel-men used to carry buggy whips with them. A stinging whip across a dog's head was apparently a very effective way of keeping dogs at bay. A better bet is an aerosol can of dog repellent. This is good only if you keep it handy and not buried too deeply in your saddle bags. The handlebar bag would be a good place to keep it.

If you do get bitten by a dog, first get some first-aid and then go to a doctor immediately. Dog bites can be very serious. Then get in touch with the police, the sheriff's office, or the dog-control officer. Call your lawyer. A dog's owner is legally responsible for the actions of the animal. If you have been bitten on a public road, you have the law on your side.

All in all, the biggest enemy of the bicyclist is heat. Heat prostration, dehydration, and leaching out of body salts can be real problems. We have covered these "staffs of life" fairly thoroughly in the chapter on backpacking. Our advice applies equally well to bike campers. Perhaps even more so.

Paved highways are hotter than lush mountain meadows. Black asphalt can heat up like a hotplate, and shoot the heat into the biker's face.

To recapitulate, drink plenty of liquids but in small and steady quantities. Take salt tablets regularly if you are perspiring a lot, or douse your food with more salt than usual. Wear a good sun hat. In really hot weather, rest or sleep in a shady place during midday. The cool of the morning and evening are better times to travel. Bikers' meals should be small, light, and frequent. It is better to eat six times a day and to eat smaller meals. Your energy requirement will be high, so eat high-calorie foods. No cyclist gets fat on the road.

The time to pitch your tent is well before dark. The place to pitch it depends on where you are. The best place is in camping parks—state, national, or private ones. Indeed, many bike campers plan their routes through areas where there are many campgrounds.

However, hitting a campground will not be possible every night. Farm or ranch woodlots or pastures are good places to camp. Do not be bashful about asking permission. If you are courteous and clean, you will be surprised how often permission is granted. As you are asking for permission, assure the farmer that you will not leave any litter and that you will not make a campfire. We have found that adult bikers are granted camping permission more readily than kids. Also, if you have dirty, scraggly hair or a scraggly beard, permission may be harder to get. The moral is: don't look like a bum. If you have long hair, make sure it is clean and well combed. If you have a beard, make sure it is neat.

If you are turned down, say goodbye politely and pedal down the road to the next farm. Sooner or later you will find a sympathetic farmer. This is part and parcel of bike camping. Despite its ups and downs, it's a lot of fun.

CHAPTER 17

Escaping to the Wild

For some of us, only wild places and wild things can mend the soul from the buffeting of our over-mechanized, over-sophisticated and, at times, nerve-shattering world. Yet, "to get away from it" is not a new phenomenon. Peace, solitude, and unspoiled nature have been a centuries-old quest of prophets, poets, and philosophers, as well as countless hobos and hermits.

A couple of years ago, we were camped at an end-of-the-road camping park. Beyond the boundaries of the park, a Canadian wilderness lay open for several hundred miles, right up to the tide-washed coast of Hudson Bay. Aside from the odd Cree Indian trapper, almost no one ever ventured there, and even the trappers were there only in winter. During the summer they lived at the mouths of the big rivers flowing into Hudson Bay. There were six of us in the party and we were using the park as a jumping-off point for a wilderness canoe trip of a week's duration. As we assembled our gear the morning of our departure, another camper joined us at the beach. During our brief conversation, he said, "My wife and I are looking forward to going on camping trips like yours, but we can't right now because our kids are too young."

"How old are your children?" one of our partners asked.

"Seven and nine," the camper replied.

"I don't know what's stopping you," our partner replied. "We're taking along two kids, twins of five."

The man was speechless. He thought we were inconsiderate as to the health and welfare of the children. But this is not so. Kids like to camp. They think it a big adventure, and a wilderness camping trip is so much more of an adventure. As for the health and safety of the children, they are in no greater danger on such a trip than the adult members of the party. In fact, children are less likely to suffer a misadventure than adults. Not only is someone supervising them more closely than usual, but everyone becomes more cautious about white water and steep hillsides. Moreover, a sick or injured child can be carried out much faster and more easily than a sick or injured adult.

One disadvantage of having small children on a wilderness camping trip is that they cannot carry their own load. Nor can they walk as fast or as far as an adult. This means that the trip must be scaled down to a level where you and the kids can cope. It may mean a certain amount of sacrifice on your part, but then having children has always meant a certain amount of sacrifice. There are limitations on wilderness camping with children, but not as many as most parents think.

The Mode of Travel

There are a number of ways that a camper can travel into wilderness areas. The mode of travel depends on a variety of factors—time, money, personal inclination, terrain, and even the age and health status of the camper.

Generally, wilderness begins where the roads end. This eliminates the car. Even a four-wheel-drive vehicle is out because it needs roads or at least flat terrain. A 4x4, as four-wheel-drives are frequently called, can, of course, get you deeper into the bush over roads where an ordinary car or pickup truck could not travel, but the only place where it could carry you into the wilderness as such is Africa and possibly the deserts of the southwest and of the Middle East.

A canoe or a sturdy pair of boots are traditional ways of getting into wild places. What other ways are there to reach the wilderness? Horseback is one. A seaplane is another. A boat is a third. In winter, skis, snowshoes, and snowmobiles can be used.

There are not many rivers in North America where a boat can be used for a wilderness camping trip. The headwaters of the big rivers flowing through Canada's north are possibilities, but taking enough gasoline is a problem. One would have to use a large boat, and big boats cannot get through the rapids and shallows of the headwaters. Some of the untamed western rivers have potential, but they are rubber-raft propositions rather than boat trips.

The best places for boats are the upper Great Lakes, Lake Superior in particular, and the eastern shore of Lake Huron's Georgian Bay. These areas are good and readily accessible. The north shore of Lake Superior has miles and miles of wild coast, but at the same time there are enough settlements and tourist establishments where gas and oil can be purchased. Of course, anyone venturing on such a trip should still take a good quantity of extra gas and oil along. Probably the rivers of South America offer the best potential for traveling through wilderness by boat. The rivers are big and deep. They can easily accommodate a launch.

One of the good things about a boat-camping trip is that it is comfortable and leisurely. Even someone too old for the rigors of backpacking or canoe tripping can go on a boat-camping trip. Also, a boat camper can take more gear and a bigger tent, which make for more comfort.

The easiest way to reach the wilderness is by seaplane. An hour's flight can carry the camper deep into the wilderness, a hundred miles from the nearest inhabitant. The camper can take with him a fair amount of gear for a comfortable stay. He can even bring in a canoe or a light car-top boat strapped or lashed to the aircraft's pontoon.

Such a camping trip, of course, requires lakes. Most of northern Canada and Alaska are full of them. The Canadian provinces of Quebec, Ontario, and Manitoba are particularly well suited for this type of trip. Not only do they have many lakes, but nearly every town has a bush-flying service with charter aircraft. There is also no shortage of lakes or charter aircraft in Alaska.

Flying deep into the northern Ontario bush for a week of fishing or camping is a popular undertaking. We know many charter-flight operators and bush airlines offering relatively inexpensive package trips for as low as $85 per man for a party of three. The costs depend primarily on the flying distance and whether the operator checks in during the middle of the week to see that all is in good order. Costs also depend on the services that the outfitter must provide. Some outfitters offer nothing but the flight, while others have tents already pitched, firewood cut, dishes, naphtha stoves, and lanterns already there on the camping site, a boat or a canoe, and sometimes a small outboard motor to use for fishing. All the camper brings is his sleeping bag, his groceries, and personal items. Most package trips of this nature, however, include only a good wall tent and a canoe or a light boat. The camper brings the rest—stoves, lanterns, ax, groceries, sleeping bags, fishing tackle, and personal gear. If you ever decide to go on such a trip, ask the outfitter if life preservers come with the canoe. Not all outfitters supply these, so you may want to bring your own.

Flying in to a wilderness area does not mean that you have to stay at a base camp. You can fly in and canoe or backpack out. We have done a number of canoe trips where we have been taken into the headwaters of a wild river and from there have canoed back to civilization. The good thing about a trip like this is that you can arrange to fly in so that your canoe trip will take you downstream. This makes paddling a lot easier.

We know of people who have been flown in to high mountain lakes and dropped off with backpacks. From there they have hiked out. In this way, one does not have to cover the same trails twice, which makes the trip much more interesting.

The other virtue of fly-in trips is that they save time. A week's backpacking or canoe travel will not take you very far if you have to make a circular route to return to your jumping-off point, usually a camping park or a lodge where you have left your car. But a week's travel in one direction allows you to cover quite a distance.

One of the traditional ways of reaching the wilderness is on horseback with a string of packhorses following behind with your gear. Riding through valleys and over mountain trails is an unforgettable experience. Anyone who likes camping and the outdoors owes himself a trip like this at least once in his lifetime.

A packhorse camping trip is a unique way of seeing the wilderness.

Packhorse-camping trips are only done in the west and, to a limited degree, in the southwest. There are a number of ways of doing such a trip. A group of campers can hire an outfitter with a pack string to take them into the mountains and drop them off. Then, after a prearranged interval, the outfitter comes back and picks up the campers. Big-game hunters frequently arrange such trips.

The campers are then free to fish, hike, and enjoy the wilderness on their own. On such a trip the campers generally supply all their own gear and grub, although some outfitters already have tents erected at a good campsite.

The other way to handle such a trip is to hire an outfitter with a string of packhorses and saddle horses, as well as a guide-horse wrangler who stays with the party. If the group is big enough, there might also be a guide or two and a cook. The outfitter provides everything—dishes, food, and miscellaneous gear. All the camper brings are his sleeping bag and personal items.

This type of trip is particularly good for tyros. The guide keeps them from getting lost and takes them to places of local interest—areas where wildlife is abundant, secret little trout streams, mountain meadows where alpine flowers bloom, scenic vistas, and trail rides.

This is also a good trip for older people. Everything is taken care of. Even the horses are saddled. And should anyone fall sick, there is someone to help. Having a cook is one of the best aspects of a trip like this. When you get back to camp in the evening tired and hungry, dinner is already waiting. Some camp cooks turn out superb meals on their old sheepherder's stoves. Surprisingly, such trips are not unduly expensive. Prices begin at about $35 per day and go up to about $50.

There are horseback outfitters in all of the western mountain states from New Mexico right up to Montana and including Alberta, British Columbia, and the Yukon. The tourist development departments in each state or province have lists of such outfitters.

In essence, wilderness camping is not radically different from camping in a park. It only takes a little more careful planning. If you forget something, you have to do without it. The camper needs to be a bit more experienced and a bit more self-reliant in terms of outdoor skills and equipment. No one should venture into the wilderness without being adequately dressed. If you use medicines, bring an ample supply split between two different bags or packsacks. The same goes for a spare pair of eyeglasses. A comprehensive first-aid kit is, of course, a must. A pocket survival kit is a must, as is a good knife. Perhaps the most important item of all is a good compass and, if you are on your own, a topographical map of the area.

Maps and Compasses

Experienced woodsmen—trappers and guides—rarely ever rely on a compass. But they generally know the country and they have an uncanny sense of direction. The lay of the land and inconspicuous landmarks are imprinted in their minds as a result of many years in the bush or mountains. This is something that most urban dwellers never acquire. We just do not spend enough time outdoors.

Compasses are available in a variety of designs and various grades of sophistication. Sophisticated compasses can be used for navigation and surveying. The best type of compass for an outdoorsman is the type where the needle floats in oil to dampen its swinging and the housing has sights for taking headings. Sylva and Suunto make compasses in this class.

All magnetic compasses react to iron and steel magnets, including those on other compasses. If you are carrying something made of steel—even a belt buckle or a sheath knife or something in a backpack—the needle can be thrown off. Run a check on this by placing the compass on a low stump and walking away a few steps, giving the needle time to come to a full stop. As you turn, watch the needle to see if it swings towards you as you approach. If it does, there is something on you that is causing the needle to deviate. You must get rid of it whenever you take a compass reading.

Learning to use a compass is not difficult. For elementary direction finding, just wait for the needle to stop, turn the dial until the north arrow and the needle are aligned, and then use whatever bearing will take you to your destination. This technique works only when the objective is large, such as a railroad or a river or, when the distance is short.

For more sophisticated compassing, such as finding a bay on a small lake many miles away, a map will be needed and the compassman will have to compensate for declination—the difference between the position of the true north and the magnetic north in degrees. Every topographical map and marine map gives declination in degrees east or west.

Topographical maps are a tremendous asset on any wilderness camping trip. A topographical map shows the features of the land—the topography —not just the roads and towns. It also shows the type of vegetation, streams, springs, swamps, ponds, and lakes, plus old logging or mining roads, railways, power lines, mining and lumber camps (even abandoned ones), cabins, and farmhouses. By studying a topo map, you can get a good idea of what to expect and what the country looks like.

The key to using a topo map lies in learning the symbols and codes. They tell the story of what actually lies on the ground. The scale of the map can vary, but the larger the scale the more detail the map will show. The most useful scale is the 7½-minute quadrangle series. The scale on such a map is approximately 2000 feet to the inch.

In the Appendix, we have given addresses of places to obtain topographical maps in the United States and Canada. You first order an index sheet of the state or province for which you want maps. With this index, you will get instructions as to how to select and order the maps that you need. Topographical maps are quite inexpensive, but be sure to allow at least four weeks for delivery. Plan your trip early and order your maps well ahead of time. Topographical maps for national parks can be purchased over the counter at all park headquarters. Topo maps for national parks can also be ordered from the United States Forest Service, Regional Centers.

File a Flight Plan

Just as aircraft pilots file flight plans, so should every camper. No one should venture into the wilderness without telling someone, and preferably two or three people, where they are going and when they intend to return.

If you are hiking or fishing in the wilderness out of a main camp, tell your partners in which direction you are going. If you are going on a wilderness canoeing trip, tell the forest ranger or local game warden when you expect to be back, with instructions that if you are two days late to organize a search.

If you are camped alone and are going out for a day's hike, leave a note at your campsite stating where you are going and when you expect to be back. If you have driven to a spot to fish or hike for the day, leave a note on the windshield of your car.

File a personal flight plan. It can save your life.

CHAPTER 18

Camping in Winter

"My favorite kind of winter camping is on a beach in Florida," a woman once told us at a party. Although that was not the type of camping we had been discussing at the time, the lady's remark was not at all facetious. A big portion of this continent never gets any snow; some of it does not even get freezing temperatures in winter, which means that the camping season does not have to end in the winter just because you do not like snow.

Florida offers much better weather, in our opinion, in January and February than it does during the hot and humid months of summer. The deserts of the southwest are also at their best. Large stretches of the Pacific coast, from southern British Columbia to California, never get any snow. Winter camping, particularly backpacking along the beaches, is only now being discovered. Hawaii has much to offer, both for the backpacker and the automobile camper.

Mexico has tremendous camping opportunities. Highway 15 along the Sea of Cortez is a prime example. Starting at Puerto Penasco, one can camp all the way to Mexico City and right to the southern end of the country. Besides visiting such fine resort cities as the beautiful Guaymos and the charming Mazatlan, the camper can stop off at countless small fishing villages and coastal towns. Highway 15 flanks the sea most of the way right down to Mazatlan. There are many camping parks and beaches open to camping along the way.

Baja California is also open to campers, with Highway 1 stretching down the entirety of the peninsula. The country is a little rougher here, and to get into some of the out-of-the-way places, a four-wheel-drive vehicle is needed. Fishing is excellent, as is swimming.

Camping in the south or southwest in the winter is no different from camping further north in the summer. For this reason, this is not what this chapter is all about. Here we will introduce you to camping in the snow.

The World of White

By and large, campers retreat and advance as the snow advances and retreats from the northern portions of this continent. Only a few have discovered that camping does not need to end simply because snow has covered the ground. The winter woods have a charm of their own. Somehow many wild creatures take on a tameness that they do not have in summer. For them, winter is largely inhospitable, a season of survival. But this is not the case for the modern camper. There is no need for any real discomfort while camping in winter, and the snow offers many activities that are not possible during the remainder of the year.

Essentially there are five methods of transportation for the winter camper: automobile, snowmobile, snowshoes, cross-country skis, and ski-equipped aircraft. Automobile camping in winter is much more restrictive than in summer. The car in winter is used to transport the camper to a jumping-off point where he will ski, snowshoe, or snowmobile out. Many of the state and provincial parks are now open in winter to snowmobilers. Some even have snowmobile trails laid out. Such parks make excellent bases. The roads are plowed after every snowfall so that cars can be driven in. All the camper has to do is park his car and head out. Or, he can pitch a tent in the park and use it as a base for shorter day trips on skis, snowshoes, or snowmobile in the surrounding countryside.

Using ski-equipped aircraft to get into the wilderness is no different from using pontoon-equipped aircraft for the same purpose. Lakes are used as landing fields during both summer and winter. In winter, snowshoes or cross-country skis replace the canoe and hiking boots.

Frankly we have not heard of anyone flying out in winter just to camp. The trip has always been associated with ice fishing on remote lakes or with winter photography. But there is no reason why a snowshoer or a cross-country skier could not be dropped off by aircraft just for the pleasure of winter camping. An interesting way to set up such a trip would be to fly in and then showshoe or ski out.

Snowshoeing

In the boreal regions of the world, the invention of the ski and the snowshoe must rank higher in importance than the discovery of the wheel. They made permanent settlement of the northern regions possible, or certainly less precarious. They enabled man to expand and inhabit areas where the snow depth presented an impossible barrier to successful hunting and food gathering.

Snowshoes have some advantages over cross-country skis. They are better in thick forests overgrown with underbrush and in terrain that is rocky and rough, like much of Canada's Pre-Cambrian Shield. Secondly, learning to snowshoe is very simple. All you have to do is strap them on and walk. Snowshoeing is also less arduous than ski touring.

Snowshoes are superior for carrying heavy loads and for walking, because the hands are free. A snowshoer can also pull a toboggan or a sleigh loaded with gear. A toboggan will hold as much gear as two men can backpack, but only one man is needed to pull it. Carrying your gear on a toboggan is

Cross-country ski touring has brought new dimensions to the out-of-doors. One of these is winter camping.

simple; loading the toboggan is even simpler. Put your gear on, cover it with a tarp or ground sheet, and lash the load down. Take turns pulling the toboggan, while the free man breaks the trail. Bring along an extra coil of rope so that two people can pull the toboggan up hill and track it down hill.

Lastly, getting equipped for snowshoeing is cheaper than getting equipped for ski touring. A good pair of snowshoes can be purchased for $20 to $30. Harnesses cost about $8. The only other equipment needed is suitable footwear. Shoepacks with rubber bottoms and leather uppers are good; insulated rubber boots are also good; and best of all are felt-lined snowmobile boots. Boots for snowshoeing should have low heels or, even better, no heels at all.

Another piece of equipment that might prove useful is a snowshoeing staff. A ski pole makes a good staff. In hilly country, an ice ax with a long handle and a ski-pole basket at the bottom is a good bet. It can serve as a pole or as an ice ax. For traveling on slopes over crusty or packed snow, crampons are useful. They can be put on and taken off as needed, just like automobile tire chains.

Clothing is the same as for any other cold-weather camping. Wool and down are best. The rest of the camping equipment is the same as any backpacker's, but a rucksack, with its low center of gravity, is better than a backpack for carrying gear.

As far as snowshoes themselves are concerned, we think that the ones with wooden frames and webbing of synthetic fiber are the best bet and the best value. With care, they will last a long time. Aluminum or magnesium snowshoes are also excellent. They are light and sturdy, but also very expensive. The plastic ones leave us cold. Some are almost useless, being too slippery, and even the better ones are not made for serious snowshoeing.

For all-around snowshoeing, the Algonquin style, sometimes called the Maine or Michigan model, is probably best. The Bear Pan type is best for very thick forests, while the Pickerel, sometimes called the Alaskan or Yukon, is best for open country. The size of the snowshoes depends on the snowshoer's weight, including his load.

SNOWSHOE SIZE GUIDE

	Weight of the Snowshoer (pounds)	Approximate Snowshoe Size (inches)
Bear Paw	110-130	13 x 32
	130-160	13 x 34
	160-180	14 x 34
	180-200	15 x 34
	200 plus	15 x 36
Algonquin	90-130	12 x 42
	130-160	12 x 48
	160-190	13 x 48
	190-220	14 x 48
	220 plus	14 x 52
Pickerel	110-140	10 x 48
	140-180	10 x 56
	180 plus	12 x 60

Do not scrimp on harnesses or bindings. Get good ones. They should be fully adjustable and sturdy.

Cross-Country Ski Touring

In less than a decade, ski touring has mushroomed into one of the most popular winter sports. Anyone who loves the out-of-doors in winter will enjoy ski touring.

Cross-country skis have some advantages over snowshoes. They are just as silent as snowshoes, perhaps even more silent. They allow the traveler to move faster and to cover more ground. They are a more exhilarating and a graceful form of travel. However, the winter camper intending to travel on cross-country skis will have to use the lightest of backpacking equipment and carry only freeze-dried foods to keep his load to an absolute minimum.

Ski touring is a far cry from downhill or alpine skiing. The techniques are different. The equipment is different and much less expensive. A ski tourer can equip himself relatively cheaply. We have seen boots, bindings, skis, and poles sold as sets for as little as $55 this past winter, but $100 is a more realistic figure.

As for the techniques of ski touring, they are more complex than those of snowshoeing, but a few hours of instruction will teach anyone the basics. After that, it's just a question of hitting the trails and toughening up the muscles. For those who do not want to take formal instruction, there are a number of fine inexpensive paperback books on the market that describe the techniques very well.

Clothing for ski touring should be light. Knickers are generally used as trousers, but light woollen pants are just as good and probably more versatile. A sweater backed with a nylon shell is excellent. While on the trail, the exercise will keep you warm. But when you stop to make camp, a down jacket or sweater will be handy. Long underwear might be useful as well.

The only specialized item of clothing used by ski tourers, besides knickers, is anklets or gaiters to keep the snow out of boots. Ski-touring boots, incidentally, do not resemble alpine ski boots. They are lower and more flexible. They look like soccer boots without the cleats.

One of the charms of snowshoeing or ski touring is the silence. For this reason, snowshoers and ski tourers prefer to head into terrain too rough for snow machines or into wilderness areas where snowmobiles are not allowed.

Snowmobile Camping

The snowmobile has revolutionized winter outdoor recreation throughout the northern portions of this continent. But, unfortunately, snowmobiling (or perhaps more correctly snowmobilers) has had growing pains. Harassment of wildlife, destruction of young trees, cutting of wire fences, trespassing on private property, and littering, have been problems. The snowmobile itself is an inanimate object, neither good nor evil. It is the machine users that create the problem.

Fortunately in the last few years snowmobile enthusiasts have been showing signs of maturity. Through public education, the formation of snowmobile clubs, and the establishment of snowmobile trails, the misuses and poor outdoor manners of snowmobilers have declined.

Even the noise level of snowmobiles is on the decline, largely due to legislation. Noise has at times been associated with power, and in both respects—noise and power—the snowmobile industry has not shown much responsibility. High horsepower ratings have been widely promoted. Yet machines with lesser horsepower ratings are safer and offer just as much fun. They are also cheaper. We do not intend to write a treatise on snowmobiling. There are a number of fine books devoted to this subject. Our main interest is to show that the snowmobile can be a very useful vehicle for winter camping. We admit to a preference for snowshoes and cross-country skis, but we use a snowmobile as well. A snowmobile can carry us into the backwoods within a few hours over a distance that would otherwise take days. Then we can camp and use our camp as a base for snowshoeing and ski touring to points of interest. The snowmobile enables us to pitch a camp by remote lakes so that we can enjoy some largely unexploited ice fishing.

The best thing about the snowmobile is that one can tow a trailer with kids and equipment. Small children can be a nuisance on a snowshoe or ski-camping trip, but not so with a snowmobile. No snowshoer or ski tourer could ever backpack the amount of gear that a snowmobile can handle—a good-sized tent, heater, lantern, two-burner stove, and sundry other gear.

Needless to say, any snowmobile trip into the wilderness should never be tackled with a single machine. Two machines should always be used, and three are better. Snowmobilers should carry a tool kit including a spare drive belt, sparkplugs, a plug wrench, an adjustable wrench, pliers, screwdriver, electrician's tape, the owner's manual, and a tow rope.

Other essential items are: a good pair of snowshoes, an ax, a good knife, a first-aid kit, and a survival kit. On a long trip, an emergency fuel supply is necessary. A light-weight block and tackle with up to 50 feet of rope may spell the difference between being stuck or going on.

Snowmobilers, including children in a tow sleigh, must be well dressed in snowmobile suits with helmets, face masks, and warm mitts. Tinted, shatterproof snow goggles are a must. Thermal underwear may also be needed. The wind-chill factor is high on a fast-moving snowmobile. Of course, if you intend to snowshoe or ski tour, lighter clothing will be needed as well. Snowmobile suits are too warm for these activities.

Long snow safaris offer some of the best potential for snowmobile camping. One of the most interesting snowmobile safaris that we have heard of was one in northern Ontario where a group of five traveled through the Canadian wilderness from the mining city of Timmins right up to Moosonee on the James Bay coast. That's the kind of winter-camping potential that snowmobiles have.

The Snow Camp

The mercury may have dipped well below the zero mark and the woods around you may be crackling from cold, but in your tent you will never feel it. Cold alone is not the winter camper's enemy. The enemy is the wind.

A windy vista is ideal for a spring or summer camp. It not only cools, but blows the bugs away. However, in the eye of winter, the wind bites through everything. So pitch your tent so that it is shielded from the wind as much as possible. Avoid lakeshores, riverbanks, and ridges. The ideal place to nestle a tent is in a thick grove of trees, preferably conifers. Pick them low and thick. Avoid tall trees that hold snow. The heat from your cooking fire may melt the snow enough to bring it all down. More than one tent has been flattened this way.

The ideal place to pitch a tent is a cosy little nook behind a ridge or on a bank where young spruce trees are coming up. A cedar swamp is also good as long as the ground is frozen. You may have to clear a space big enough for your tent and perhaps a short path to the outside, but the winds will not reach you inside. This is why deer yard up in cedar swamps.

An alpinist will not have much choice. He will be well above the tree line, but there is nearly always a lee spot somewhere to be found. A pile of snow will help to break the wind, but don't pile the snow against the tent. A piece of tarp or a ground sheet can be used to provide a windbreak. Snow can then be piled against it to hold it down and provide a barrier.

The alpine camper's biggest concern is the avalanche. If he is still below the tree line, he should avoid pitching camp on slopes that are denuded of trees. A forest fire may have been the cause, but it could have been an avalanche. A smaller avalanche can bury a skier or a tent and a camper without knocking down any trees. Avoid steep slopes—anything over 25 degrees gradient.

Your tent should always be pitched on the snow. Never clear a spot for a tent, because frozen earth feels like ice. Snow is warmer. We have learned that the hard way. If you can put down some other insulation, so much the better. A bed of evergreen boughs is excellent. And, as we said earlier, there are still places in northern Canada where a camper can do this without feeling guilty about the damage he has caused.

A ground sheet of extra-heavy canvas is almost as good and a lot faster to put on. A backpacking snowshoer or a ski tourer may not be able to lug one, but a snowmobile camper can always find room for it, even if he has to fold the ground sheet over the sheet of his machine and ride on it. A plastic sheet comes as a poor third, but it's better than just the tent floor. Plastic has the advantage of being much lighter and more compact than a tarp. Winter backpackers take note—pack the plastic out or burn it when you break camp!

Another advantage of a ground sheet or a bed of boughs is that the tent floor will never freeze to the melting snow below. Some melting always occurs below the tent as the temperature warms up, particularly in heated tents. The crunch comes in the morning when you want to break camp and find that your tent is frozen to a mass of hard snow below. Pulling and tugging may tear the tent loose, but it also may rip the tent, particularly the seams in the floor.

Many books on camping recommend steaming the tent loose. We have tried it but it does not work too well. It would take clouds of steam. A faster and easier way is to cut a sapling pole and run it under the tent to break up the snow. Once the tent is free, the chunks of snow and ice that adhere to the bottom can be knocked and brushed off. If you have a strong ground sheet, you do not have to worry. Pulling is unlikely to rip it. A sheet of plastic can be cut and ripped loose.

Some summer-camping techniques, such as pegging down the tent, have to be abandoned in winter. Pegs won't hold in snow. In snow, deadmen of logs are used. Short chunks of rope are run over the grommets and tied to a log. The log is buried and snow is packed over it. If you are expecting a real blizzard, pour water over the packed snow and let the deadmen freeze in. Smaller deadmen are used for guys and other ropes. Trees and bushes can also be used to anchor a tent. The next job is to pile snow up on the tent's snow valances, if the tent has them. Do not go beyond eight inches. If you are using a full-length fly, you can pile snow around it for about a foot. Tents designed for winter camping nearly always have flies.

The best tents for winter camping are the self-supporting ones that need no pegs. Thermos, Bauer, Bishop, and Eureka all make them. The last three make true alpine tents that have tunnel entrances, cook holes, and other features.

A Bag Full of Tricks

Snow camping has its own tricks and tips. Some of them, like leaving nothing lying about, we learned the hard way. It's easy to lose things in the snow. Skis should always be stood up, perhaps impaled in a snowbank. The same goes for ski poles. Snowshoes, on the other hand, should be hung up, out of harm's way, and away from gnawing porcupines if the webbing is made of real rawhide babiche. Porkies do not like synthetic webbing or oil-treated leather.

The snow around the doorway or tunnel to the tent should be well trampled down. A few evergreen boughs or a piece of tarp as a mat is not a bad idea. The tent, of course, should always be pitched on a bed of well-trampled snow.

To enter the tent we generally back into it, keeping our feet outside and knocking the snow off before coming in. Some snow, however, is always tracked in. We keep a terrycloth rag and a small sponge handy to mop up any water.

We sleep with our boots. Yes, you read the last sentence right, but we do take them off. We wipe our boots and dry them completely, then put them in a plastic bag at the bottom of our sleeping bags. We do not like getting into cold boots in the morning.

We never go on a winter-camping trip without two pairs of sunglasses. Polarized glasses are best. On bright days, the danger of snow blindness is very real. Lip balm is another must. Chapped lips are even more painful in winter than in summer. Spare mittens or gloves are also necessities.

Incidentally, tents do not have to be heated in winter. If you are well clothed and well fed, you do not need a heater. A backpacker might not be able to cope with one. On the other hand, a heated tent is very pleasant. You do not have to bundle up as much and, if some of your clothing gets wet, you have a way of drying it.

Catalytic heaters are best for winter camping. They are flameless. They do not use much oxygen or release much carbon monoxide. Carbon monoxide can be far more dangerous than frost. A rested man will never freeze to death. The cold will wake him. But even a rested man can be poisoned by carbon monoxide. Whenever you have the heater going, make certain that the tent has plenty of ventilation. Never go to sleep with the heater on.

We also take plenty of reading material along for winter camping trips— a couple of heavy tomes. Heavy, in this case, does not refer to weight but rather to literary context. *Gone With the Wind*, *War and Peace*, and *Origin of the Species* can all be purchased in paperback editions. Avoid the quickies that you can polish off in two or three hours of steady reading. Winter gales and blizzards have been known to blow for days. Cards and small compact games, including miniature chessmen and checker sets, can also be useful to while away the hours. Do not rely on conversation to keep you from boredom. Have you ever tried to talk steadily for two days?

Cooking in the Snow

Our first bit of advice will be on cooking snow. Yep! Cooking snow. That is how you get water on many winter camping trips unless you are willing to chisel a hole through the ice. Melting enough snow for drinking, cooking, and dishwashing is fairly time consuming. The way to begin is to melt a little at a time over low heat until you get half an inch of water in the bottom of a pot. This will keep the pot from scorching. Then fill up the pot and pack the snow down. The packed snow will eliminate or reduce evaporation from the pot as the snow is melting. Remember, it takes a bucket of snow to make a cup of water. Ice melts faster and gives more water, so use it if you can get it.

Cooking in winter requires a greater release of heat. The colder it is, the harder the stove has to work and the longer it takes to boil the billy. If you can lay some insulation down under the stove—a few evergreen boughs or a piece of canvas—more heat will be released upwards. Cooking at high altitudes compounds the problem, as we have already explained in Chapter 6.

Precooked foods are a good idea. Stews, beef hash, and chili con carne, to mention a few, can all be cooked ahead of time and frozen in plastic bags. All you have to do is pop the contents into a pot, melt it, heat it up, and your meal is ready. Freeze-dried foods are also good. Meat can be "half cooked." Steaks should always be precut into individual pieces. Why? Because hacking up frozen meat is a thankless task and most camping skillets are not big enough for big chunks of steak.

Remember that winter camping uses up a lot of energy. Bring plenty of calorie-laden food. A house with a burning furnace is always warm. Your stomach is a furnace, and your body is the house.

CHAPTER 19

Making a Camp

When the tent is pitched and the camp is made, the camper has a home. It is unnecessary for us to give directions as to how to pitch a tent. For one thing, with the scores of different tents on the market today each requiring a slightly different technique, we could fill an entire book on just how to pitch tents. Every tent comes with a brochure that describes in detail how to pitch it. Read it carefully and then have a practice run in your back yard before taking off to your favorite camping spot.

However, there are many other things that go into the making of a camp. Here are some of them.

Choosing a Campsite

The prime requisite of any campsite is a piece of flat ground for the tent, and a cooking space. A camper can make do with nothing more. But anyone who has made a dry camp in the desert or high up in the mountains knows what it is like. We all take water for granted until we don't have any. A dry camp can be an ordeal. At the very least, it is inconvenient. A source of water near the campsite is therefore an important requirement. We will have more to say about water later.

Another requirement may be firewood if you are not packing a gasoline or a propane stove. This means that you must camp in a forested area or along a treed river course or lakeshore. It's surprising how often these requirements—flat ground, water, and firewood—are not easy to find, particularly in mountain country.

The automobile camper will find the task of choosing a campsite simple. Campsites have already been made for him unless he is camping on the side of the road on public land. The most difficult thing for a car camper in a campground is to find a pleasant location, one that is perhaps close to the beach or a bit secluded and away from noisy campers. Do not pick campsites near the main campground roads or you will be bothered by late comers and other night riders. It is also a good idea to pick a site near the water taps, showers, and toilets if you have small children. You will use a fair amount of water, and kids simply "have to" at the most awkward hours.

The wilderness camper has other things to consider. For example, if he is on a horseback trip, then a lowland meadow or a slope with good pasture is a must, even if he has brought along oats for the horses. A boat camper will need a sheltered cove to beach or anchor his boat. For the canoe tripper, a smooth shoreline is ideal. Certainly having to wade through ankle-deep water and calf-deep mud to beach a canoe is no fun. And even the automobile camper on public land needs a good firm parking place that will not turn into mire should it rain for a day or two. Shade for the car is nice as well.

In desert country, camp should never be made in dry water courses. If a rain did come, the water would flow in torrents. Flash floods are the rule after a rain in arid countrysides. These are very dangerous.

When selecting a campsite, avoid low ground if at all possible. Depressions get more dew, more fog and, in the fall and early spring, stronger frosts. But the biggest problem is drainage. After a day-long rain, you may find that your tent is standing in a pool of water.

If you like to explore old mines, abandoned logging camps, and ghost towns, remember that such four-footed beasts as pack rats, skunks, raccoons, and porcupines frequently make their homes in and below such buildings. Thus, it is wise not to camp too close. Camping in tall grass also has its problems—ticks, chiggers, and mosquitoes live in it. Swampy meadows are prime mosquito habitat.

Before pitching your tent, remember that mosquitoes breed in stagnant water and blackflies breed in running rills. During the peak bug season, try to camp some distance from both. Also, look around for such things as hornet nests in trees, yellowjacket nests in holes underground, and even wild honeybee hives in hollow trees.

A good campsite should be selected partially on the basis of anticipated weather. During the summer the campsite should get the morning sun for warmth and to dry the dew. Besides, the morning sun is cheerful. As the sun rises and the temperature with it, you will want your tent to be shaded by trees. A part of the campsite should always be open to the sun in case you have clothing, dishes, or anything else that needs to be dried.

A good place to pitch a tent is on the east or north-east side of trees. Big boulders, rocky bluffs, ridges, or ledges can also be utilized to provide shade by pitching the tent on their north or northeast sides.

Wind direction is an important consideration. In cool weather, try to pick the lee side of rocks, trees, or bushes. In mountain or desert country where gale-force winds can strike, pitch your tent behind a ridge, a boulder, or anywhere else where it will be sheltered from the blasts. In cold weather, wind pierces through everything.

On the other hand, during the sultry days of summer, a breeze is

Choosing a campsite takes a bit of know-how, but the prime requisites are a piece of flat ground for pitching a tent and some cooking space.

welcome. If your tent has windows, be certain that in the summer they face the prevailing winds. Your campfire also has to be sheltered from the wind. During the height of the mosquito and blackfly seasons, a breezy ridge or a point on a lake is nice. A zephyr tends to keep the bugs grounded.

It is unwise to camp or park your car under dead trees or live trees with large dead branches. If a windstorm comes up, it may bring the trees or branches down on top of your tent or car. Dead trees in wind can be very hazardous.

We always try to pitch our camp in a spot with a good view. We avoid disrupting the environment around us as much as possible. We dig out rocks and stubs only when absolutely necessary. We never camp in the middle of an alpine meadow. The soil is too shallow and the vegetation too fragile. A week of camping there may leave a scar that will not heal for several years. We camp on the edges of meadows where trees and bushes grow.

Water, Water Anywhere

The automobile camper pitching camp in a campground has it easy. The water comes from a tap, just as at home. All he has to do is carry in a bucket or two to his camp. The canoe tripper also has it easy. He is on water all the time. And if he is deep in the wilderness, the water is probably pure enough to drink just by dipping in. However, in deserts or in high mountain country, the camper frequently must pack his water in. In such camps, water is precious and is never wasted.

Except in very arid country, finding water is frequently not difficult. Certainly the lack of water is generally not a problem in the forested regions of this continent. A topographical map is a big help. It shows every water course, pond, and swamp. If you do not have a topo map, remember that water flows downhill, so the places to find it are valleys and gorges.

Vegetation may provide hints to the water supply. A row of willows or alders may mean a stream. A row of cottonwoods may also mean a water course, but whether it will have any water is another matter. Remember, even dry water holes or depressions in water courses may have water below ground. Dig down a few feet and find out.

In dry country, birds and mammals may provide a clue as to the whereabouts of water. Watch for flights of doves in the late afternoon when they normally go to water. Desert quail also troop to water in the afternoons. If a profusion of deer tracks all heads in one direction, there may be a waterhole there.

If you are planning to camp in dry, hot country, remember that you may need as much as four or five quarts of water a day. Take that into account when deciding on how much you should bring. Water purity is a frequent concern to novice campers. There are still many places on this continent where the water is safe to drink by dipping it from a stream or a lake. The water from little brooks and rills in mountain country is usually safe. But the tentacles of pollution are reaching farther and farther into the wilderness every year. So, if you are uncertain about water quality, you have no choice but to boil it or treat it.

Halozone tablets are a convenient way of purifying water. One tablet per pint of water is adequate in most cases. In some cases, two may be needed. The water will taste of chlorine, but you have no choice. Aerating it by pouring it between two containers will remove some of the taste. Some of it can also be disguised by using powdered or crystallized drink mixes or instant tea with lemon.

If you ever run out of halozone, a few drops of household bleach such as Javex will also purify water. Two or three drops of iodine from your first-aid kit into a quart of water will do the same trick.

Boiling water can be a chore. It is time consuming and uses up a fair amount of fuel. If you are on a canoe trip and there is plenty of dry driftwood around, fuel will be no problem. Otherwise it may. Water also takes a long time to cool before you can drink it. We tend to drink lots of tea. In this way you do not have to wait for the water to cool, but there are only so many mugs of tea a day that a person can stand. And besides, on hot muggy days, only a cool drink brings refreshment. The ultimate decision of when to boil, purify, or drink the water as it is can be made only by you.

Sanitation

The old cliché about cleanliness being next to godliness must have been first coined by a camper. To leave a messy, littered campsite or mountain trail is desecration of nature. In some ways it is too bad that a camper does not require a license with a loss of camping privileges for a period of time should he leave his campsite a mess. On more than one occasion, we have cleaned up a mess left by someone else. It is not a pleasant chore, but someone has to do it.

Again, the automobile camper has it easy. All he has to do is deposit his trash in the garbage bin provided by his campsite. But there are no garbage cans in the wilderness. The rule today is that if you brought it in full you can pack it out empty. Older books on camping recommend flattening tin cans and burying them. Only half of this advice is acceptable today. Flattened cans take less space in a backpack than full ones. If backpackers today still buried cans along the trails, there would be mounds of bare earth near every campsite. Besides, cans are not biodegradable in a short space of time. Burning paper and similar trash is still permitted, but metal and glass containers must certainly be packed out.

In many of today's parks, no one is allowed to camp within 100 feet of water. It's a lamentable fact, but camping pressure in some places is such that water has to be protected from pollution. Only biodegradable soap should be used for washing clothing and dishes.

In remote Canadian canoe country, it is still permissible to carry one's washing to the riverbank and wash it by beating the clothes against rocks. But this practice must be condemned elsewhere. In the more popular camping parks, clothes should be washed in a wash basin and the water poured out 200 feet from a lake or stream.

Latrine pits should never be dug closer than 200 feet from water. If you are going to be camping in one spot for a long time, bring a small bag of lime to sprinkle into the latrine after each use. If you do not have lime, then a bit of loose earth is the next best bet.

Simple toilet facilities can be made by digging a latrine pit between two trees and then lashing a couple of sapling poles to the trees over the pit to act as a seat. A third pole, a little higher up, can serve as a back rest. This kind of toilet can be made only if you are camping in a wilderness area where a camper can cut down poles without feeling quilty. Incidentally, an empty tin can over a roll of toilet paper will keep it dry and prevent it from unraveling in the wind.

While on the trail, a camper should bury his wastes in a shallow pit. The same goes for dog wastes. A small folding shovel or a stone-mason's trowel is a handy tool for this.

One thing is certain. Children should not be allowed to "go behind the tent" just because father or mother find it inconvenient to go out with them in the middle of the night. As we said earlier, taking children camping bears certain responsibilities. These include teaching the proper attitudes about our natural environment.

CHAPTER 20

Fires and Firewood

A campfire has an aura about it that no stove can ever match. The flames and fragrance of a wood fire stir in us feelings from our racial youth. It was not just tools that separated us from other creatures, but rather the use of fire.

There are still large tracts of wilderness on this continent where wood is free for the taking. Only dead trees should ever be burned. Most campers find fallen trees more convenient, and they certainly should be utilized if they are dry. Along the lakes and river shores of northern Canada, there is generally plenty of driftwood.

In many cases, a camper who intends to make a fire must first obtain a fire permit from the nearest forest ranger's office. This fire permit may not be granted if the woods are very dry and the forest fire hazard is acute. In fact, we have seen the fire hazard so high that vasts tracts of woods were closed to the public. We trust that every camper knows enough to completely douse a campfire with water when he leaves camp. The ashes should be soaked until they are cold to the touch.

Fireplaces

The first secret of making a good cooking fire lies in the fireplace. A camper can build several types of fireplaces, depending on terrain, weather, prevailing winds, and the length of time he will be using the campsite. The best fireplace is one with a high back for draft and wide arms for pots and pans, plus a metal grill or grate. This type of fireplace can be constructed only if plenty of the right kind of rocks are available.

Another good type of fireplace is the keyhole or flask-shaped ring made of rocks. The fire is maintained in the main portion of such a fireplace. Hot coals are periodically raked under the grate into the narrow lower portion of the fireplace for cooking. A third type of fireplace is a double row of rocks about a foot apart, with the fire between the rows of rocks. A grate is then placed over these rows to support cooking utensils.

A trench fireplace is a good bet if no stones or rocks are available. You must, however, dig deep enough to get into mineral soil, and the depth also depends on the size of the fire. The trench fireplace should be dug in the shape of a narrow, army foxhole. It must be narrow enough for a grate or grill, and the open end should be upwind. A more sophisticated version of a trench fireplace incorporates a small hole upwind which is connected with the fire pit. As warm air rises from the fire, cooler air comes into the fire pit through the hole and assures better combustion.

And to make things really simple, a fireplace can even be made out of two logs—preferably green hardwood logs. The logs are simply laid parallel to each other about a foot or so apart, or are laid in the form of a narrow "V". The V-shaped fireplace is better on windy days in open country.

For a quick pot of coffee or bowl of soup, an open fire is generally adequate if there is no wind or if the fire is sheltered from it. Three rocks can be used to support the coffee pot or small saucepan, as can three metal pegs. The pot or pan can also be suspended over the fire with two sapling forks and a crossbar. Do not try to get a perfect fork; such forks are hard to drive into the ground. Select a sturdy sapling with a strong off-shoot branch. Such a crotch is easier to sink by hammering on the main stem. The forks and cross piece should always be cut of green wood if possible.

The Right Woods

The second "secret" to a good camping fire is the selection of the right wood for the task. For example, if you want to broil a steak, you will need hot coals from hardwood such as hickory or hard maple. On the other hand, if you want a pot of tea in a hurry, your best bet would be to use a quick-burning softwood like poplar. Of course we realize that in many situations the camper will not have a choice. He must use whatever dry, dead wood is available.

Botanically, trees are divided into two groups—the coniferous evergreens and the broad-leafed deciduous trees. Forest workers generally refer to all deciduous trees as "hardwoods" and to all conifers as "softwoods." This nomenclature is not wholly accurate. There are many species of "hardwoods" that do not have hard wood. The poplars are a good example. All of the conifers, however, do have soft wood.

The camper must divide his trees by density and texture of the wood. Let us begin with the softwoods.

Coniferous Softwoods

The *balsam fir* lives on moist bottomlands from Newfoundland to northern Alberta and south through the northern Great Lakes region to the Atlantic coast. The balsam fir is very soft and resinous, with a high moisture content when green. Hence it should be used only when seasoned. When dry, it burns quickly and throws fast heat. It spits and snaps while burning, so be careful. The balsam fir is basically a wood for quick cooking. Small, dry, pencil-thick branches make good kindling, even when broken from a live tree.

The *red, white,* and *western red cedars* are the only cedars that are of importance to the camper. However, cedars as a whole are only third rate as campfire woods. White and western red cedars live on moist sites, while red cedar prefers open areas. As a group, cedars are widely distributed over North America. All cedars are light, soft woods that burn poorly while green. When dried, they ignite and burn quickly but give off a lot of smoke. Again, sparks pop and fly when cedar burns, so a campfire of cedar must be in an area well away from debris and humus. The bark of cedars, when dry and shredded, makes very good tinder for starting fires.

The *Douglas fir*, a large western evergreen, is not really a fir. This relative of the spruces ranges from southern British Columbia to central California and east to Montana. It is suitable as a campfire wood only for quick boiling, as it is soft and light, burns quickly, and tends to be smoky.

The *pines* are found over most of North America on sandy soils. They are light and soft. White, red, jack, and lodgepole pines burn well even when green. Pitch pine has to be seasoned to burn well. Pines are easy to ignite and throw a surprising amount of light. They are good woods for quick cooking, but they too tend to pop and throw sparks. They also blacken cooking pots, so if you are using pine as a campfire wood, coat the outsides of your pots with soap before you put them onto the fire and you will have an easier cleanup.

The *spruces* are a widely distributed group of trees. White and black spruces range from the Atlantic to the Pacific, from Alaska to the Great Lakes. Western white, Douglas, Englemann, and Sitka spruces are found in the west, while red spruce is found from Nova Scotia through the New England states to central Ontario. The spruces are light and soft, and should be seasoned to be good campfire woods. When dry, they start easily and thus make excellent kindling. They do not burn as fast as some of the other softwoods, hence they are a better bet for all-around campfire cooking, as long as hot and long-lasting coals are not needed. Small dead branches of standing spruce trees make good fire starters, even in wet weather. Again, the spruces throw sparks.

The *tamarack*, sometimes called the larch, is the only conifer that sheds its needles each fall. There are several species of larch belonging to the pine family. Tamaracks, however, make much better firewood than pines. Tamaracks range from Newfoundland north to the Yukon and south to the Rocky Mountain states, the Great Lakes states, and into New England. The tamarack lives on moist, boggy soils. It is the heaviest and densest of all the conifers, but still is best used when seasoned. Many north woods campers prefer tamarack for firewood over all species except white birch. Tamarack burns with a strong and even heat, and is fairly long lasting. It does not, however, leave the coals of birch. When burned green it spits and sputters.

Deciduous Softwoods

The *alder* is a tree of the swamplands and stream bottoms from Alaska to the Gulf Coast, from Newfoundland to the midwest, and from the Rockies to the Pacific. Alder is a fast-burning wood, with a strong heat and quick flame. It tends to spit and snap and burns out quickly. It is an excellent wood for quick boiling and cooking, as well as baking. Because it burns fast, you must have plenty of it cut ahead of time. When well seasoned, it makes excellent kindling.

The *basswood*, or linden as it is sometimes called, is very light and soft. It is found from Maine to the Dakotas and from southern Ontario to Kentucky. Before being used in a campfire, it should be well seasoned. Basswood burns quickly and turns to ash readily. It too, spits, snaps, and throws sparks. Like all softwoods, linden is good for boiling and quick-cooking.

The *poplar* family, a large groups of trees, includes the aspens and cottonwoods. All of these are rapid growing trees, some species being the first to re-colonize old burns. Some poplars grow on high, dry, sandy soils. Poplars range from Newfoundland to Alaska through the Rocky Mountain states, the Great Lakes, into New England, and south to Kentucky. Poplar woods are light and soft. They burn quickly when dry, and are good for fast-boiling and cooking. When dry, poplars make good kindling.

The *sweet gum* is a beautiful bottomland tree growing from Connecticut to Florida and west to Texas. Its wood is not as soft as some of the other softwoods, but it burns quickly and is thus best used for quick-cooking.

Deciduous Hardwoods

The *ashes* comprise about 15 species of deciduous hardwoods in eastern North America. They range from central Ontario to British Columbia and south to Florida. Red, white, and black ashes are most often used as campfire woods. These are heavy hardwoods. They do not make good kindling because they tend to start burning slowly. White ash can be used green, but red and black ashes should be seasoned first. All ashes throw good strong heat and produce coals that are ideal for broiling and frying.

The *birches* make excellent firewoods. Black and yellow birch are superior to white birch. However, trappers in northern Canada depend on white birch to heat their cabins throughout the winter. The black birch is found from southern Maine and southern Ontario to northern Alabama, along the Appalachian Mountains. The yellow birch ranges from New England to Minnesota and from central Ontario south to Pennsylvania. The white birch, sometimes called the paper or silver birch, is found from Alaska south through Canada and the Great Lakes region to the Atlantic coast. All birches are hard and heavy and burn well even when wet. They start readily and burn slowly with an intense flame. The coals retain heat for a long time and are good for frying a steak or simmering a stew. The bark from all birches can easily be stripped off and makes excellent kindling.

Beech will burn when green and give off plenty of heat. It is a very good hardwood. It ranges from central Ontario to the Gulf of Mexico and from Maine to Kansas. Many outdoorsmen consider beech as good as oak for campfires because the coals retain heat for a long time.

The *hickories* are all excellent campfire woods. The shagbark is the best of the hickories, and there is no doubt that hickory is the finest of all campfire woods. Hickories are found in a variety of forest habitats, and their general range runs from Maine and southern Ontario south to Louisiana and Texas. Sawdust and chips from hickory are the best wood to use for smoking fish, ham, or bacon. A hickory-smoked ham has a flavor all of its own. A steak broiled on a thick bed of hickory coals is far superior to charcoal-broiled steak. Hickory burns with a hot and steady flame, and the coals remain hot for a long time.

The *hornbeams*—both the American and the hop—are very hard and heavy woods. The hop hornbeam is sometimes even called ironwood. The hornbeams range from southern Ontario through the eastern half of the United States to northern Florida. They do not burn too well when green, but when well seasoned, burn with a steady heat and produce hot coals.

The *maples* are a large group of trees encompassing over 20 species in North America. Only the hard or sugar maple, however, makes first-rate firewood. The sugar maple is a very hard wood, and burns evenly even when green. It produces very hot and long-lasting coals for long cooking or broiling tasks. The soft maples such as red maple burn much like poplar.

Fishing and hunting guides, like these Cree Indians, generally know how to make a good campfire and cook over it well.

They are good for quick-cooking. However, they should not be used unseasoned because they do not burn very well when green. How do you tell a soft and hard maple apart? By the leaf margins. The lobes on the leaf of a soft maple are serrated or saw-like and the underside of the leaf is silvery green. The hard maple, on the other hand, has smooth leaf lobes and the underside of the leaf is a dull green.

The *oaks* constitute about 60 species of deciduous trees in North America. Most of them make good firewood, but some must be seasoned first. The best oak is probably the white oak, which will start well and burn even when green. The red and water oak, on the other hand, should first be seasoned. The oaks are all hard and dense woods that burn slowly and strongly, producing hot coals. The only exceptions to this are the willow oak and the scarlet oak, both of which burn quickly and can be used for quick-boiling, while the other harder oaks are good for long-cooking and broiling.

Campfire Cooking Tips

For someone who is used to cooking over a stove, or even a camp stove, a campfire may seem a bit perplexing because of the problem of regulating heat. This is a problem, and the cook must recognize that cooking over a campfire requires constant vigilance. The food must be checked faithfully to ensure that it does not become overcooked or, even worse, burned.

However, there is an approximate way of determining the temperature of a fire. This method will give you a temperature of a fire plus or minus ten percent. Hold your open palm in the same spot over the fire where a pot will be placed and begin to count—one thousand one, one thousand two, one thousand three, and so on, to achieve one-second intervals. If you can hold your hand over the fire for only the first count, your fire is over 500 degrees F. If you can keep your hand there for two or three seconds, you have a fire of about 450° F. Four or five seconds, 375° F, and six to eight seconds about 300° F.

Fire-Starting Basics

Now that you know how to build a fireplace and choose the right wood, how does one start a fire? All it takes is a clump of dry tinder, a couple of handfuls of kindling, and a small armful (8 or 10) of medium-sized sticks of firewood. The tinder, kindling, and firewood should be as dry as possible. The fire is built in three layers, starting with the tinder and ending with the sticks of firewood.

There are a number of good tinder materials. Dry, loosely crumpled paper is one of the best. Most campers have some paper scraps from food wrappers and containers. Wax paper and paper milk cartons make excellent tinder.

Bark from dry birch makes good tinder as well. So does shredded bark from cedar or sagebrush. Dry grass and leaves can also be used, but they are less efficient. If tinder is not available, a fuzz stick—simply a dry, softwood stick from which very thin slivers have been shaved to form a feathering effect at the end like a feather duster—is a traditional fire-starting trick.

If you lack tinder, make certain that your kindling is very thin and highly flammable. A candle may help to get the fire going. Small pieces or squares of fire starter such as are used to start barbecues are also very good.

Some campers splash a bit of gas, lighter fluid, or charcoal starting fluid on to their tinder and kindling. It is up to you, but we have never found it necessary. On rainy days, though, it may be handy. If you are going to use these volatile fuels, strike the match after the container is sealed and put away. We think that fuels of this sort gradually trap a camper into using less and less tinder and kindling and more and more fuel. Eventually he will find that the fuels will not help him to start big sticks.

Kindling can be any small sticks, with diameters running from pencil size to finger thickness. Small, dry twigs and branches from any evergreen or poplar tree make good kindling. Sagebrush makes good kindling. If you have to chop up kindling, use the dry center core of the tree. The initial sticks of firewood can be any dry wood, depending on what is available or handy.

The match or light should always be put to the bottom of the tinder from the upwind side. The wind will whip the flame up through the tinder, creating a bigger, hotter fire for the kindling to catch. Starting the fire the right way is just as easy as starting it the wrong way, and much more efficient.

Tyro campers usually think that starting a fire in rain or snow is difficult. It is not, but special precautions have to be taken. If the ground is very wet or covered with snow, lay a foundation for the fire of dry firewood, bark, rocks, or even a few dry evergreen branches. Stack these up tepee-style, using very dry kindling from dead twigs of evergreen trees. These will stay dry even during a severe rainstorm. Keep your tinder in a dry place until the last minute. If possible, use a natural overhang such as a rocky ledge under which to build the fire. A canvas tarp or even a poncho can be used to shelter the fire until it gets going.

Finding a dry striking surface for your matches is not at all difficult. Two strike-anywhere matches can be struck together. A button or metal zipper can also be used to strike the match. In rainy weather, special waterproof matches are a great asset.

One last tip about fires. Keep them as small as possible for the task at hand. A big fire is not always the best to cook on, and it requires a lot of wood. We prefer to spend less time chopping and gathering wood and more time enjoying the outdoors.

CHAPTER 21

What's for Dinner?

"What's for dinner?" and "What time's dinner?" are two of the most persistent questions asked of the camp's cook. "When's dinner?" for most campers is an easy question to answer—almost all day long! The out-of-doors really burns up calories and stirs up appetites, and a lot of campers eat and snack off and on all day long. As we mentioned in the chapters on backpacking and canoe tripping, light meals and snacks many times a day are the ideal way of keeping the stomach satiated yet not overloaded. But even automobile campers build up hefty appetites swimming, hiking, exploring, chopping firewood, and busying themselves around the campsite.

As for "What's to eat?" that depends largely on what facilities are available for transporting and storing foodstuffs. Wieners and beans sure taste great over a campfire in the evening, but there is no way a backpacker can haul heavy cans and perishable ground meat up the trail for any longer than the first day or two.

The automobile camper has more versatility because he can transport storage and refrigeration facilities with him and can stop along the road from time to time to stock up. Similarly, the boat camper can replenish his supplies at marinas and store his perishables in a cooler. Try to purchase most of your staples at your supermarket before leaving home. Small country stores are usually quite expensive.

Although the cooking facilities somewhat regulate the type of meals that can be turned out, with the proper ingredients, the auto camper can produce Cordon Bleu camp dinners every night. The backpacker is a little more restricted.

Provisions for the Pantry

Meat is the staple of most North American diets. Meat is a problem or at least an inconvenience on many camping trips. It spoils rapidly, especially during hot weather, and ground meats go "off" even faster than solid chunks of meat. Meats are also heavy to carry. One salvation on the meat scene, however, is the hard, spiced, salami-type sausage. Although still heavy, these sausages will keep almost indefinitely without refrigeration and can be eaten either out-of-hand or in soups, stews, or many other taste-tempting dishes. Most European delicatessens carry a variety of such salamis. Never pre-slice the salami before your camping trip. It defeats the purpose of having a whole piece away from drying air and bacterial infestations.

Slab or side bacon is also a good bet for the camp trail. Although it does not last as long as salami, smoke-cured bacon (the real thing—not artificially hypodermic syringe-smoked bacon) will keep for weeks without refrigeration. The fat from it can be used for other cooking chores. When solidified, it tastes great on fresh pan-fried bread after a long day of hiking. To keep non-smoked bacon from molding, wash it in vinegar and brine before you leave home. Then wrap it in cheesecloth (not tinfoil or plastic—raw meat has to breathe) and try to keep it out of the sun.

Some of the pre-cooked, compressed meat sticks sold in supermarkets (and given out in taverns so you will down more drafts) are also good on camping trips. They can be kept almost indefinitely without special care. When space and weight permit, canned meats such as corned beef and chicken are an excellent choice.

For the first night or two out in camp do not hesitate to bring along that thick, juicy steak for the barbecue grill or, better yet, that big chunk of ribs for the barbecue spit. It's a great way to start a trip, and the leftovers will be good with eggs in the morning.

Fats for cooking are perplexing to novice campers. What to cook with? What to spread on bread and toast? Bacon grease is a good all-around bet for cooking. It keeps longer than either butter or margarine. However, butter tastes better on flapjacks and makes better wild blueberry tarts. Thus, for a lot of campers, tinned butter is the solution. Butter in cans will keep until the can is opened, and then for some time thereafter if kept either in a refrigerator or in the shade. Campers who are advocates of the school of polyunsaturated fats can bring along Gerry polytubes filled with peanut, sesame, or corn oil. The camper with a cooler, of course, can get away with keeping margarine on ice for weeks on end.

Dairy products are also a problem to tyro campers. They need not be, because the automobile camper can cope with them quite easily in his cooler and the backpacker can take them in other-than-fresh forms. Cheese is one of the most nutritious of the dairy products and has very good storage qualities. Hard, unsliced cheese can be kept fresh for long periods of time simply by keeping it in a plastic bag out of direct sunlight. It does not have to be refrigerated. Should it begin to mold, simply scrape the mold away. It will not do you any harm.

The most convenient way to take milk along on a camping trip is in the dried form. At that statement, most campers immediately screw up their noses and say "yech"! Actually, dried milk is not all that bad, particularly if it is

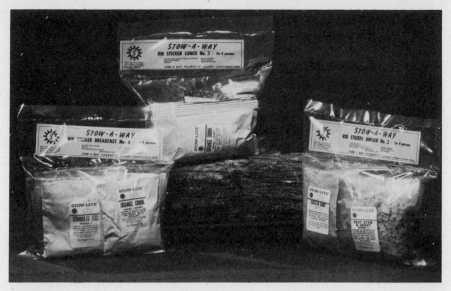

The camper's menu is dictated largely by the facilities that are available for transporting and storing foodstuffs. The automobile camper is lucky. He is seldom far from a store. But even a backpacker can eat well thanks to light-weight, freeze-dried package meals.

left to sit until the milk crystals dissolve and, if possible, cooled before drinking. If you do not have a cooler, try to keep your milk supply in a jar or jug supported between rocks in a cold, quick-flowing stream of water. If you have brought a bottle of wine along to go with your steak that is a good way to get it cooled too. Powdered whole milk can be purchased in camping supply stores and sometimes in larger drugstores that deal with formula needs for infants.

Eggs are one of the best ways to start a camp morning, but they present transportation problems. Fresh eggs are the best, and can either be packed in specialized crush-proof containers or left in the polystyrene containers they come in from the supermarket. Fresh eggs can also be broken and stored in a thermos bottle, and then poured out when needed. Eggs do not, however, keep as long once they have been cracked. Dried eggs are the solution to all this, but then dried eggs just do not have the flavor of fresh eggs. However, once they have been incorporated into pancakes or muffins, you will not really be able to tell the difference.

Fish is another good source of vitamins and protein on camping trips. Freshly caught brook trout or jumbo yellow perch, pan-fried on the shore for lunch, are certainly hard to beat. But you cannot always count on the fisherman in the family to bring home the dinner. Canned fish is really quite heavy to bring along, although canned tuna and salmon are favorites with many campers. Dried shrimp and other dried seafoods are lightweight, nutritious, and great for backpackers. With rice and freeze-dried vegetables, they are a treat.

Bread is one of the staples of a camper's diet. The best breads to bring along on any trip are the very heavy, dark European breads that are wholesome and nutritious. Because they are so dense, one slice is very filling.

The alternative to bringing bread is to make your own. The camper's great standby is bannock, or frypan bread. This is very simple to make and very nourishing. It is a real delight with butter and jam. If you make a batch in the evening, with a big frypan, it will give you enough for the next day's lunch as well. To make bannock in a small frypan, preheat the pan and grease it lightly. In a bowl or another pan, mix together 1 cup all-purpose flour, 1 teaspoon baking powder, and ¼ teaspoon salt. Roughly cut in 1 teaspoon bacon grease, butter, or margarine. Then stir in enough cold milk (about a third of a cup) to make a stiff dough. If you do not have milk, water will do. Place the dough in your pre-greased frypan so that it is about an inch high. If you like your bread crusty, make a couple of holes in the center of the dough. After dusting the loaf lightly with flour, hold the skillet over low coals to brown the bottom of your bannock evenly. Then prop the pan at an angle to catch the front of the fire to brown the loaf. When the loaf has a hollow sound, about 15 minutes from the time you first put it on, you will have some of the best camp bread ever.

Biscuits and muffins are also popular. For the automobile camper, packaged muffins in a reflector oven are easy to whip up. Small rolls can also be made from the bannock recipe, and commercial powdered biscuit doughs make good, nutritious eating in camp.

Pasta is another camp staple. Give beans a try on camping trips. There are a great many varieties of dried beans and peas on the market that keep without any refrigeration at all and are not excessively heavy to carry for the nutrition and bulk that they provide. Homemade baked beans in camp taste like nothing you have ever had out of a can.

The "Instant" Revolution

Although you may turn your nose up at them in your kitchen at home, instant and freeze-dried foods have been a great boon to the backpacker and canoe tripper. Freeze-dried beef stew does not exactly taste like Mother's, but it is nutritious and energy-generating when on the trail. It is also convenient and weighs next to nothing. Freeze-dried foods are largely prepared foods with all of the water removed. In many cases, this saves from 70 to 95 percent of the total weight involved in the meal. You need only water to reconstitute freeze-dried foods.

Instant foods such as mashed potatoes, oatmeal, gravies, and puddings are quite palatable and provide good nutrition and variety on the camping scene, as do dried soups.

For dessert, instant puddings, dried fruits, fresh fruits, hard candies, and nuts more than fill the bill.

Most serious backpackers make up "gorp" for quick energy snacks. The recipe for gorp varies from hiker to hiker. Here's one that we use: mix together one pound of raisins, ½ pound of chocolate bits, ½ pound of shelled hazelnuts, ½ pound of shelled walnuts, and ½ pound of chopped dates. Pack this mixture into plastic bags to munch along the trail. Gorp tends to make you a bit thirsty, so do not use it for hiking in desert country.

Cooking in the Out-of-Doors

Anyone who cooks on the stove at home knows how to handle a frying pan and a saucepan. However, for the mountain hiker and backpacker, high altitudes, with their lack of oxygen, present special problems in both boiling and baking. The following table should help.

COOKING GUIDE FOR HIGH ALTITUDES

Baking	
Altitude (feet)	*Decrease in Baking Powder Required*
3,000	10 per cent
6,000	25 per cent
10,000	30 per cent

Note: If eggs are called for in a recipe, add one extra for altitudes of 9,000 feet and over.

Boiling	
Altitude (feet)	*Increase in Cooking Time Required*
3,000	20 per cent
4,000	30 per cent
5,000	40 per cent
6,000	50 per cent
7,000	70 per cent
8,000	90 per cent

Note: At altitudes higher than 8,000 feet, a pressure cooker is handy and saves a lot of cooking time.

CHAPTER 22

Beasts, Bugs, and Itchy Plants

The wildlife makes the out-of-doors a live and vital place. To see a moose belly-deep in water munching on water lilies in a remote lake is an unforgettable sight. A mountain slope without wild sheep is just a landscape, regardless of how scenic. Even a little chipmunk picking up crumbs around the campsite table adds to the outdoor atmosphere.

Wildlife is one of the main attractions that draws people out-of-doors. One good example of this are the "wolf howls" organized by park naturalists in Ontario's Algonquin Park. Hundreds of people come from hundreds of miles away just to listen to wolf packs howl on a quiet summer night.

However, the camper must realize that some creatures can be pests, nuisances, and even dangerous. For example, we have had porcupines chew our ax handles and canoe paddles; raccoons raid our food supply; and even mink steal our fish. One learns to cope with such nuisances quickly. The place to keep axes and canoe paddles is in the tent or in the trunk of the car, or perhaps hung up in trees (not near the trunks of trees because porcupines are largely arboreal).

Food should be hung up or locked up in a metal ice chest or wooden box or, even better, kept in an automobile. Certainly no camper should leave food lying about. Throwing food scraps into the bush is not recommended, even in wilderness areas. It attracts masked bandits such as the raccoon, who may not be satisfied with just crumbs. But no one should mind sharing his catch of fish with a mink, particularly if one can get a good look at it.

Deer on the Highways

As surprising as it may sound, one of the greatest hazards facing the automobile camper, in fact any motorist traveling in big-game country, is big game on the highways. Automobile collisions with deer are unbelievably common, but elk, moose, and even bear represent hazards as well. For example, in the relatively small state of Pennsylvania, about 25,000 deer are killed annually by cars. That is more than are harvested by hunters in many other states. But Pennsylvania is not unique. Texas has about 16,000

Bears are a potential hazard to any outdoorsman, but unprovoked attacks are rare. Every camper should, however, exhibit caution and common sense when camping in bear country.

deer-car collisions every year; California, 8000; and Michigan, about 7000. The province of Ontario reports about 125 car collisions each year with moose and 40 with bears. Many of these are fatal to the car's driver and passengers. A moose is a big animal to hit.

A camper driving through big-game country should do so defensively. A deer may leap out in front of your car at any time. If you see a deer on the side of the road, slow down. Always obey all deer-crossing signs. They were put there for a purpose. A deer may be walking up the middle of the road just around the next bend. If you come across an animal on the road at night, turn your headlights off momentarily, leaving only your parking lights on. Chances are that the animal may be mesmerized by the beam of your headlights and a millisecond of darkness may be enough for it to jump out of the way.

If a collision seems unavoidable, do not try to swerve to miss the animal. If you go into a spin and lose control, you may hit something much more formidable—a rock or a tree. In such a case, it is best to hit the animal straight on. If you do hit a big-game animal, treat it like any other accident and report it to the police. Even if the damage to your car is negligible, report the accident to a conservation officer. If the animal was not killed instantly, a game warden will want to track it down to prevent further suffering. Above all, do not go near a stricken animal. Wounded deer, bear, or moose can be very dangerous. Let a police officer or conservation officer deal with the animal.

Beware of Bears

There are three species of bears on this continent—the polar bear, the grizzly bear, and the black bear (which incidentally can also be brown or cinnamon in color). The Kodiak or brown bear of Alaska is considered by most zoologists to be a geographic race of large, coastal grizzlies.

All bears can be dangerous, but the grizzly is probably the most dangerous of all. He is big and can be aggressive. Grizzlies have been known to attack even when unprovoked. Backpackers asleep in their sleeping bags have actually been killed by grizzlies. Sows with cubs are more prone to attack than lone bears. Should you ever get between a sow grizzly and her cubs, she is almost certain to attack. But a grizzly at a food cache, such as a winter-killed elk carcass, is also dangerous. If the bear thinks that you are about to steal his food, he may come at you.

Polar bears can also be dangerous. This is largely because they seldom see humans. In the Arctic, the polar bear is the biggest animal on land. Everybody fears him, and he seems to know this. The only thing that the polar bear fears is dogs and now, the drone of an Eskimo's snowmobile.

Polar bears and grizzlies will both raid food caches. However, they are not the raiders that black bears are. This, of course, may be because they are not as numerous as black bears and because they live in areas where large numbers of people do not travel.

If you are venturing into bear country, be especially observant. When you come across a bear, give him a wide berth. Go ahead and watch him, but from a safe distance and with binoculars. When traveling in the grizzly country of the western U.S., western Canada, or Alaska, wherever possible use binoculars to glass the countryside before walking through.

If you are traveling in very thick cover, make a lot of noise as you walk along. Some hikers carry tin cans with gravel in them to rattle or sheep bells to jingle, but talking, singing, or whistling will do. Nearly every bear will run if he gets a chance. When walking in thick cover, such as on a forest trail, keep your eye out on the trail for grizzly tracks. If fresh tracks are present, be especially cautious.

The black bear seldom represents any real danger. Unprovoked attacks are very rare. The blacky is just not an aggressive individual. However, sows with cubs have been known to attack people when they thought that their cubs were being threatened. But they can be such a nuisance. We have had them raid food supplies and even break into our tent. We have had them steal moose meat from us. They raid garbage containers and panhandle in many of the national parks. The danger is that these half-tame bears have no natural fear of humans. A number of campers have been hurt or mauled while trying to feed or play with them.

Incidentally, if a bear suddenly rises on his hind feet ahead of you, he is standing up to get a better look—not to charge. Both grizzlies and black bears have very poor eyesight. They always charge on all four feet. Nearly always they begin their charge with a roar. Their lips are furled and their jaws are wide open, and there is no mistaking their intention.

Never think that you can outrun a bear. Bears can run with incredible speed, faster than a horse for short spurts. Climbing a tree is good defense against a grizzly. A mature grizzly cannot climb trees, but a black bear is an agile tree climber. The old trick of playing dead when being mauled by a bear does work. In a number of cases this has saved the life of the victim. The potential danger should not deter anyone from venturing into bear country. If you exhibit just a trace of caution and common sense, the danger will be absolutely minimal. Walking across the average city street presents far greater dangers than camping in bear country.

Rabies Is on the Increase

During recent years, the incidence of rabies has increased dramatically. This phenomenon may be cyclic; the increase may also be due to the increased numbers in recent years of small carnivorous animals. We now have more coyotes, foxes, skunks, and raccoons than we had a decade or two ago. There are two reasons for this: first, our farmers and departments of agriculture have become more enlightened and no longer hire poisoners to kill these creatures; and second, few men earn a living as fur trappers any more.

A rabid animal is dangerous. The most common symptom of this disease is unusual behaviour—a fox running towards rather than away from you; an animal acting sick or stupid. If you encounter such an animal, stay away from it. Keep your kids and dogs away from it. If you have a firearm, shoot the animal but not through the head. A veterinarian will need the brain to determine whether the animal really was rabid. If someone is bitten by a wild animal, he should see a doctor immediately. It is important to kill it so that it can be diagnosed for rabies. If the doctor does not know whether the animal was rabid or not, he has to assume that it was and must begin a series of anti-rabies injections. If your dogs go camping with you, they should be vaccinated against rabies regularly.

Porcupines and Dogs

There are not many dogs, only a few really, that just cannot resist porcupines. To these dogs the porky may seem helpless and dull-witted, but when the dog rushes in to attack, he gets a really unpleasant surprise. Imbedded quills are very painful, and can be dangerous if they are not removed immediately. Should your dog become quilled, get him to a vet as quickly as possible. If you are on a wilderness trip, you have no choice but to de-quill the dog yourself.

To do this, you will have to have someone hold the dog still. If a second person is not available, you will have to tie him. The best way to do this is to wrap him in a jacket or blanket and to tie a belt or rope around him so that he cannot hit you with his feet. Each quill must be slowly twisted out with a pair of needle-nosed pliers, starting in the chest area. Remember that the dog will be frightened and in pain, and may become a fear biter. You may have to use a muzzle or softly tie the dog's mouth with a handkerchief or a piece of soft rope. After you have taken out the quills, get the dog to a veterinarian as soon as possible so that he can administer an antibiotic to prevent any secondary infection.

Serpents

Of the 200-plus species of snakes found throughout the United States and Canada, only a few are poisonous. Yet even today, there are still ignorant people who kill every snake on sight. In our western culture, the snake is a symbol of evil. But rays of light are finally penetrating even the darkest clouds of fear and ignorance, and we are realizing that snakes are an interesting group of reptiles. All snakes, even the poisonous ones, fit into nature's scheme of things. Many perform useful roles in controlling small rodent and other pest populations.

Every camper should exercise care when camping in country where poisonous snakes are common. He should not only be able to recognize poisonous species at a glance, but should also know their habitat.

There are two families of terrestrial poisonous snakes on this continent — the coral snakes and the pit vipers. The pit vipers include the rattlesnakes, the cottonmouth, and the copperhead. A detailed description of these snakes, their geographic distributions, and their preferred habitats can be found in any reptile guide. The essential thing to remember is that the pit vipers have deep facial pits on each side of the head, halfway between the nostril and the eye. The rattlesnakes, of course, also have rattles on their tails. However, these do not always rattle before striking, particularly in cold weather. The coral snake has bands of red, yellow, and black around its body. There are other snakes with such markings, but the coral snake's key identifying feature is that its red and yellow bands touch each other.

No one should be afraid of camping in country where poisonous snakes are known to live. Snake bites are actually very rare, when compared to the host of other accidents that can befall campers. We are many thousand times more likely to be killed driving to a favorite campground than we are to be bitten by a poisonous snake. Moreover, snake bites are rarely fatal. Less than two people in every 1000 that are bitten actually die.

Any camper traveling through poisonous snake country should, however, exhibit some caution. Being observant is the first line of defense. Wearing good sound leather boots is another. If you are rock hounding or climbing, watch where you put your hands and what you grab. The same goes if you are picking berries or mushrooms. Use tools to overturn rocks and logs. Learn to recognize the buzzing rattle of a rattlesnake and even the billy goat odor that is emitted when a rattler becomes aroused.

There is a lot of controversy about treating snake bites. In the days of old, the recommended procedure was to apply a tourniquet, then make an incision around the bite, and suck the fluids from the wound. The medical profession has generally discredited this method. In many cases the treatment is worse than the bite.

Anyone subjected to snake bite should be taken to a hospital as quickly as is feasible. The victim should be kept calm and still on the way to the hospital. If the bite is on the extremities, a tourniquet can be helpful in keeping the venom contained. Make sure that the tourniquet is not too tight and that it is loosened every few minutes to allow for circulation. If a bitten extremity is kept lower to the ground than the heart, the venom will not spread as quickly.

The use of ice as a cold pack in treating snake bites is also controversial. Ice has been known to cause tissue damage and other problems. If ice *is* going to be beneficial, it is so only during the first hour or so following the bite.

Injections of anti-venom are the usual way of treating snake bite. Anti-venom (AV) is a horse serum, and its misuse can be fatal. It should be injected by a physician, but if you are camping in snake country, it is a wise precaution to take along an anti-venom kit and to get proper instructions for its use from your family doctor.

Other Reptiles

There are not very many other reptiles in North America that can cause the camper problems. There are only two poisonous lizards—the Gila monster and the Mexican bearded lizard—both found in the southwest. The bites of these lizards are seldom fatal. Other reptiles should be approached with caution. The American alligator and the American crocodile are two such animals. The crocodile is extremely rare. The alligator is much more abundant, and can be encountered in the swamplands of the south. Neither of these reptiles grows as large or is as dangerous as the African species.

The snapping turtle can also inflict a painful bite, but does so only when annoyed. Some of the larger water snakes will bite if handled carelessly. The bites of these snakes are not poisonous, but they have been known to cause nausea.

Beating the Bugs

Biting bugs of one sort or another are one of camping's biggest nuisances. However, there are ways to beat biting insects, or at least to lessen their depredation to a tolerable level. Mosquitoes and blackflies are two common pests. Mid-spring, after a short spell of warm weather, is generally their peak season. But in swamp country, mosquitoes persist all summer. Fortunately both of these insects are easy to combat.

The first and best line of defense is proper clothing. Clothing should hang loosely on the body and should be made of fairly tightly woven material.

With such clothing, the mouth parts of the mosquito cannot penetrate to bare skin. Clothing should also be light in color, as off-whites and light khakis are much less attractive to mosquitoes and blackflies than darker colors. Blackflies, in particular, are attracted to dark colors. Where blackflies are very thick, cuffs of shirt sleeves should be buttoned around the wrist and pantlegs should be tucked into boots so that the insects cannot get inside clothing.

Insect repellents are very helpful. There are a lot of different brands of these on the market, but the best we have ever tested is Cutter's. Most of them can be obtained in aerosol sprays, oils, jellies, and sticks, and all have advantages and disadvantages. Oils and jellies persist on the skin much longer than aerosol sprays, thereby giving better protection. They are also less easily washed off by sweat. Aerosol sprays, on the other hand, are convenient because they can be sprayed over clothing. If you are camping in an area where these insects are really troublesome, you may have to use a mosquito head net and even a pair of cotton gloves.

Smoke helps keep them away, and so does the wind. When hiking, stick to high ridges, open fields, and lakeshores where the wind blows stronger. Set up camp on breezy islands, open ridges, or other open areas where the wind is strong. The fly screens and sewn-in floor of your tent will keep most biting insects out of the tent itself.

Blackflies breed in running water, thus it is a good idea to stay away from the fly source when setting up camp. Mosquitoes, on the other hand, breed in stagnant water.

Other biting bugs include horseflies, deerflies, ticks, chiggers, and itch mites. Horseflies and deerflies are very aggressive and persistant insects. Loose clothing of tightly woven material is almost the only defense against them. Insect repellents are not very effective. Both these types are common in livestock-raising areas or in big game country.

Ticks are common pests in some areas. Their bite is painless, but since they live by sucking blood, they are most unpleasant. Also, they can be carriers of spotted fever, but fortunately this disease is extremely rare. Ticks are normally picked up from vegetation. They then crawl to some area of bare skin where they bite through and gorge themselves on blood. Before a blood meal, ticks are about one-quarter of an inch long, but blood-filled ticks can become several times that size. Favored areas for ticks on humans are the back of the neck along the hairline and the back of the ears. When traveling in tick country, check your clothing and your body carefully every night.

Great care should be taken in removing ticks to ensure that the body is not simply torn off and the insect's head or mouth parts left under the skin where they may fester. Ticks may be removed with a pair of tweezers in one hand and a pin or needle in the other. The pin or needle is used to pry the mouth loose. Another method of removing ticks is to coat the insect heavily with a greasy lotion, vaseline, or molten paraffin. This shuts off the air supply to the insect and forces it to let go. Burning the insect with a lighted cigarette is also effective; it can then be picked off with tweezers. Incidentally, if you have brought your dog along, examine him very carefully for ticks each evening. Dogs are very susceptible to them.

Chiggers and itch mites are generally not so prevalent as some of the other insects. They are tiny little things, almost microscopic. They live in brush and tall grass and are picked up as you walk by the vegetation. From there, they crawl into warm areas on the body such as under the arms, under a wristwatch strap, and so on.

The best way to combat these insects is to take a shower every evening if possible. If you are camping in an area where chiggers and itch mites are really bad, dust your wrists, neckline, and ankles with powdered sulfur. Keeping pantlegs inside boots may also help. So may staying away from lush stands of vegetation.

The bites of all of the insects mentioned, except ticks, itch. Swelling in the bite area is frequent. Some people react more severely to bites than others.

Ice or a cold pack can help to alleviate the swelling. Calamine lotion will help to relieve the itching. We have found that the commercial preparation, Absorbine Jr., is also good for treating mosquito bites that itch and have swollen. Both items should be included in the first-aid kit of any camper who is venturing into bug country. If you lack either of these, mix baking soda and water into a thick paste and smear it on over the bites.

Bees, Wasps, Hornets

Wasps, yellowjackets, bumblebees, and honeybees are all capable of inflicting painful stings. The venom that these insects inject is, on an equal volume basis, as lethal as that of a rattlesnake. In fact, more people die annually in North America as a result of being stung by such insects as wasps, hornets, and bees than as a result of snake bites.

The poison from bee, wasp, and hornet stings seems to have an accumulative effect. The first few stings may only bring on pain and swelling. Subsequent stings, however, may bring about such symptoms as nausea, difficulty in breathing, and even death. Some people are hypersensitive to the stings of bees, wasps, hornets, and the like.

Precaution is the best defense against these insects. Do not disturb them or their nests. Neutral-colored clothing helps. Bright colors and black attract bees, as do sweet or strong-smelling perfumes and after-shave lotion. Keep food, particularly sweet things, covered at all times, and do not leave food on picnic tables. Do not put wildflowers on your picnic table. And wear shoes; yellowjackets live in the ground. Wasps, hornets, and yellowjackets are dangerous because they frequently attack in swarms. A single wasp nest may hold 10,000 insects. Keep your kids away from such nests, because throwing rocks and sticks at them is one sure way of inviting trouble.

There are several things you can do if you have been stung. A bee's stinger may still be in the wound and should be removed. The longer the stinger remains in the skin, the more venom the poison sac will release into the wound through its hollow needle. Do not pick the stinger off, because grasping the top end where the poison sac is will result in more venom entering the wound. The best method is to scrape it off with a knife blade, a wooden match, or even a fingernail. Apply ice to the wound and keep the wound away from heat.

The sting of hornets or wasps will not leave any stinger behind. These insects do not lose their stinger and can inflict more than one sting in succession. Again, apply ice. Medical attention should be sought immediately if multiple stings have been received or if hypersensitivity to such stings is suspected.

Any camper who suffers badly from asthma or hayfever or reacts badly when stung by the common insects or by bees, wasps, or hornets should contact his family physician before leaving on a camping trip in order to acquire recommended medication as a first-aid precaution.

Spiders and Scorpions

Scorpions and black widow spiders are largely villains of B-grade movies and paperback thrillers. Bites from either are rare, and death as a result of being bitten is almost unheard of. Scorpions are nocturnal. They spend their daylight hours hidden under rocks and brushpiles. Sleeping under the stars in scorpion country may be a bit more hazardous, at least in theory, as there is a chance that a scorpion has chosen your ground sheet as an air mattress or a convenient place to hide as dawn breaks. But campers rarely sleep under the stars today.

Black widow spiders, on the other hand, are generally found in rubbish and old, abandoned buildings. A camper who likes to explore abandoned mines and visit old ghost towns would probably be wise to exhibit some caution. But again, in our opinion, the danger from black widow spiders is more theoretical than real.

A bite from either a scorpion or a spider may cause swelling, pain, nausea, fever, and even speech or breathing difficulties. The more allergic a person is to the venom, the more drastic the reaction. Children are more susceptible than adults. Anyone bitten by either of these insects should be taken to a doctor immediately. First aid consists of the application of an ice pack to the bitten area. The bitten person should be kept calm, as in the first-aid treatment for snake bite.

Stinging Plants

Poison ivy, poison oak, and poison sumac, along with stinging nettle, are four pesky plants that commonly occur in camping areas. All of these plants exude toxic chemicals that can cause anything from mild itching to severe

Every camper should know this plant—poison ivy—and keep away from it.

blistering after coming in contact with skin. In the case of poison ivy, oak, and sumac, the chemical is phenol, which is found in the sap of the plants. Hence the camper's chances of being infected are greater in the spring and early summer when the plant is growing and the sap is running. The most common way to come in contact with the toxins is to walk through a patch of plants and rub against them as they grow up trees or on fences. However, dogs often pick up the toxin on their coats and transfer it to persons who touch them. Insects pick up the poison on their feet and then land on people. Hikers pick up the toxin on their boots and pantlegs and then handle their boots.

The best way of coping with these poisonous plants is to learn to recognize them and avoid them. A good field guide to the shrubs of eastern North America should be of some help in identification.

Poisoning from any of these plants may become evident within a few hours to a few days. The most common signs are itching and inflammation of skin, followed by the emergence of water blisters. The effects of these poisonous plants are very severe on some persons, sometimes requiring hospitalization. If you suspect that you have been in contact with these plants, the best procedure is to lather with a good strong yellow laundry soap, rinse thoroughly, and repeat the procedure. If inflammation and itching still develop, see a doctor.

CHAPTER 23

A Camper's Outdoors

There is more to being a good camper than knowing how to choose a campsite, use an ax, pitch a tent and cook a nourishing meal over an open fire. A good camper must be a good outdoorsman. He should be able to identify the common creatures and plants around him. But even more important, he must understand how nature in his environment functions—what makes the old girl tick; what makes her hurt and bleed; what wounds heal quickly and leave no scars; what wounds scar or even worse never heal.

The New Awareness

Let us imagine that we are camped on a high hillside. Below us, the forested valley is a canopy of green. The forest below controls all life in the valley. As we backpacked through the valley, it was like walking through a darkened cathedral. The leaves above shut out most of the light. The forest floor was covered with leaves from last autumn. Here and there a gray skeleton of a dead tree stood upright, its naked branches looking bleak and ghostly in the half-light. A few fallen tree trunks dotted the floor, their bodies in various stages of decay.

In a few spots, where light penetrated the massive green canopy, the forest floor was covered with mosses, seedlings and saplings, each hungrily reaching for the life-giving sunlight. Some of the dead trees on the forest floor had never survived beyond the sapling stage. Such are the perils of competition. The moment a seedling sprouts, it immediately begins to compete with other seedlings for moisture, nourishment, and light. It grows as long as it has the strength to endure the competition from other trees and depredation from myriads of creatures. Organisms of all kinds use the tree for food and shelter. The tree is a host for fungi and bacteria. Insects feed on its leaves, bark, roots, and other tissues. Rodents gnaw at it. Birds eat its fruits and buds. Deer, elk, and moose browse on its green tips and shoots.

The forest and its creatures are tied together in an intricate web. The insects that feed on the trees are fed upon by birds. Some of the birds that live in the branches of the trees scatter seeds so that other trees will grow. The rodents that gnaw on the bark and shoots of the trees are in turn prey for owls, hawks, and foxes. The deer that browse on the saplings are preyed upon by wolves and at times by men. When calamity strikes one stratum of part of the forest web, the impact is felt through all the other strata.

Camping, indeed all forms of outdoor recreation today, requires a new outdoor ethic. Our pioneering age is long over. There are no frontiers left to conquer on this continent; indeed there may not be any frontiers left to conquer on the entirety of this earth. When mankind was younger and his numbers led a precarious existence in the face of nature, a state of harmony existed. This harmony did not reign in monotones but with wavelike undulations, because nature's cycles do not function like machinery or move like clockwork. Nature is not static—hurricanes blow, earthquakes shudder, floods rampage down valleys and droughts parch the land, and from all sides all living things try to use nature for their own purpose.

Nature throughout her cycles acts as the great leveler, overproducing on one hand to ensure survival of the species. And when survival is ensured, she balances the population to the carrying capacity of the land.

But throughout all of nature's cycles, things are used—molecules of carbon are converted at every step of the way. Man, being part of nature, is also a user. But today's man is strong and numerous. His strength is so great that he can level mountains, fill entire valleys, and turn wild rivers into quiet ponds. All these activities have not been done without a price.

It can be successfully argued that man's numbers have now multiplied so greatly that once again he is standing on the threshold of precarious existence. The hair-thin fractures on the porcelain-cup earth are an indication that major resources of key minerals and petroleum will not last forever. When they are exhausted, as they one day must be, we will have a world-wide crisis.

Even world-wide hunger will become a reality if our populations continue to spiral. And don't let anyone talk you into believing that miracle wheats and rices will save the day. Many of the world's undeveloped countries do not have the financial means necessary to implement the latest advances in agriculture. Even if they did, there isn't enough petroleum to be made into fertilizer and to power tractors on the scale needed to create the mythical agricultural revolution. Today, half of the world's population is suffering from malnutrition, and tomorrow will starve.

All of this will simply be an act of nature reasserting herself. Deer herds starve in overbrowsed deeryards during severe winters. This is not an unusual phenomenon on this continent. Famine is not an unusual occurrence in parts of Africa and Asia in times of drought. Both examples are acts of nature carrying out her role as the great balance wheel, bringing populations of inhabitants down to the carrying capacity of the land, of the habitat. It may be cruel, but it's a fact.

181

The New Creed

What does all this have to do with camping? Plenty. Outdoorsmen of every persuasion have always been in the forefront of every conservation movement in the world. It is the outdoorsman who first sees the transgressions. The National Wildlife Federation, the Audubon Society, the Sierra Club, and the Wilderness Society—all of them influential conservation organizations—were all founded by concerned outdoorsmen. It is imperative that anyone who loves the out-of-doors, as anyone who goes camping must, support at least one of these organizations by at least taking out a membership. Being active in local chapters, at the grassroots level, is even better.

The time has come for all of us to be very concerned with the rapacious way we are using all of our natural resources, including our lands. Developers, dammers, and logging barons are covetously eyeing our last remaining wild lands, and even our national parks are threatened by commercial developers and their pork barrel politicians with plans for ski lodges and resorts.

Man is a user, as is every other living thing on this earth, but the problem is that man has not always used with wisdom. We must use with restraint. We must apply the old adage of "waste not, want not." The opening of a new strip mine should no longer be hailed as a welcome step in man's progress. Instead, we should sing eulogies to the hillsides that will be stripped and destroyed. The dedication ceremonies for new dams should become eulogies to the once wild rivers that the dams killed.

But equally important, man must be less successful at procreating his own kind. There can no longer be any doubt that our ever increasing numbers are, at least partially, responsible for the plight of our resources. The crowding of our campgrounds is, in part, an example. The time is just around the corner when campers will have to reserve a campsite or a week on a hiking trail. It is better for 100 people to have a quality outdoor experience than it is for 1000 people to live in a tent-filled slum. The remaining 900 will have to wait their turn for next year and the years after that. Hunters, in many states, have adopted this philosophy. The demand for hunting licenses for some big game species is greater than the number of animals that can safely be harvested in a year without depleting the breeding stock. Both game animals and outdoor space are valuable natural resources.

Wisdom and restraint on the part of campers must be a part of the new outdoor ethic. Unfortunately, neither commodity is particularly prevalent among people. That's why all campgrounds have to lay down rules as to what campers may not do. That's why we have a littering problem almost everywhere we venture. These people are nothing but eco-criminals.

If a citizen is witness to a crime, he generally co-operates with law enforcement authorities in reporting the crime—giving a description of the suspect, and so on. Why should eco-criminals in our parks and wilderness areas be treated any differently? If you see someone leaving their garbage behind, report him to the park authorities. The park you will be protecting is your own.

Picking a wildflower, cutting down a sapling, making a bough bed, shooting a ruffed grouse, and leaving footprints in an alpine meadow may all be transgressions against nature, but none will leave a scar if not repeated too often. A platoon of hikers walking in line may wear a trail across a meadow. A platoon of hikers after that may break up the trail, and when the rain comes they will erode the soil.

Every spring, nature produces a new crop of saplings, more wild flowers, and young ruffed grouse. Part of that crop may be used in some places, but only in some places and only a part. The wise camper knows where and when. Alas, not all campers are wise.

It's the wise camper who realizes that camping, at least in part, is supposed to be a communion between man and the environment from which he sprung. It's a return to our racial past where every man lived closer to the earth from which he was and still is a part. The overuse and misuse of this earth affect or will affect all creatures that live on it. It is man who plays the pipes, and it will be man who has to pay the piper. The song that the piper plays depends on us.

APPENDIX

The following agencies have useful information on camping on their respective lands.

UNITED STATES

Office of Information
National Park Service
United States Department of the
   Interior
Washington, D.C. 20240

Information Office
Bureau of Reclamation
Washington, D.C. 20240

Information Office
United States Forest Service
United States Department of
   Agriculture
Washington, D.C. 20250

National Park Service Regional Offices

Midwest Regional Office,
1709 Jackson Street,
Omaha, NE 68103
Information Officer: Betty White
(402) 221-3471

Pacific Northwest Regional Office,
523 Forth and Pike Building,
Seattle, WA 98101
Information Officer: Charles Gebler
(206) 422-5201

Northeast Regional Office,
143 S. Third Street,
Philadelphia, PA 19106
Information Officer: Bob Burns
(206) 597-7018

Southwest Regional Office,
Old Santa Fe Trail,
P.O. Box 728,
Santa Fe, NM 87501
Information Officer: Frank Mentzer
(505) 982-3375

Southeast Regional Office,
3401 Whipple Avenue,
Atlanta, GA 30344
Information Officer: Jim Howard
(404) 526-7560

Western Regional Office,
450 Golden Gate Avenue,
Box 36036,
San Francisco, CA 94102
Information Officer: Ed Winge
(415) 556-5186

National Capital Parks,
1100 Ohio Drive, S.W.,
Washington, D.C. 20242
Information Officer: George
  Berklacy
(202) 426-6700

National Forest Regional Offices

Northern Region,
Federal Building,
Missoula, MT 59801

California Region,
630 Sansome Street,
San Francisco, CA 94111

Intermountain Region,
324-25th Street,
Ogden, UT 84401

Eastern Region,
633 W. Wisconsin Avenue,
Milwaukee, WI 53203

Alaska Region,
Federal Office Building,
Box 1628,
Juneau, AK 99801

Southwestern Region,
517 Gold Avenue, S.W.,
Alburquerque, NM 87101

Rocky Mountain Region,
Bldg. 85,
Denver Federal Center,
Denver, CO 80225

Pacific Northwest Region,
319 S. W. Pine Street,
Box 3623,
Portland, OR 97208

Southern Region,
1720 Peachtree Road, N. W.,
Atlanta, GA 30309

National Wildlife Refuge Regional Offices

George W. Watson,
Area Director,
813 'D' Street,
Anchorage, AK 99501
(907) 265-4868

Wilford O. Nelson,
Regional Director,
Box 1306,
Alburquerque, NM 87103
(505) 843-2321

185

John D. Findlay,
Regional Director,
1500 Plaza Bldg.,
Box 3737,
Portland, OR 97208
(503) 234-3361

Travis S. Roberts,
Regional Director,
Federal Bldg.,
Twin Cities, MN 55111
(612) 725-3500

C. Edward Carlson,
Regional Director,
17 Executive Park Drive North
   East,
Atlanta, GA 30329
(404) 633-9531

Merwin A. Marston,
Regional Director,
10597 West 6th Avenue,
Denver, CO 80215
(303) 234-2209

Richard E. Griffith,
Regional Director,
John A. McCormack Courthouse,
Boston, MA 02109
(617) 223-2961

State Camping Information

Alabama: Bureau of Publicity & Information, Room 403, State Highway Building, Montgomery, AL 36104.

Alaska: Division of Lands, Department of Natural Resources, 334 Sixth Avenue, Anchorage, AK 99503.

Arizona: State Parks Board, Room 431, Capitol Building, Phoenix, AZ 85007.

Arkansas: Publicity & Parks Commission, State Capitol Building, Little Rock, AR 72201.

California: Division of Beaches & Parks, P.O. Box 2390, Sacramento, CA 95811.

Colorado: Colorado Game, Fish & Parks Department, 6060 Broadway, Denver, CO 80216.

Connecticut: State Park & Forest Commission, Hartford, CT 06115.

Delaware: State Park Commission, 3300 Faulkland Road, Wilmington, DE 19808.

Florida: Development Commission, 107 West Gaines Street, Tallahassee, FL 32304.

Georgia: Department of State Parks, 7 Hunter Street, S.W., Atlanta, GA 30334.

Hawaii: Hawaii Visitors Bureau, 2270 Kalakaua Avenue, Honolulu, HI 96815.

Idaho: Department of Commerce & Development, Room 108, State House, Boise, ID 83707.

Illinois: Department of Conservation, 102 State Office Building, Springfield, IL 62706.

Indiana: Tourist Division, Department of Commerce, Room 334, State House, Indianapolis, IN 46204.

Iowa: State Conservation Commission, East 7th and Court Avenue, Des Moines, IA 50309.

Kansas: Park & Resources Authority, 801 Harrison Street, Topeka, KS 66612.

Kentucky: Department of Public Information, Advertising and Travel Production, Capitol Annex, Frankfort, KY 40601.

Louisiana: Tourist Development Commission, P.O. Box 44291, Baton Rouge, LA 70804.

Maine: Department of Economic Development, State House, Augusta, ME 04330, or Forestry Department, State House, Augusta, ME 04330.

Maryland: Department of Forests & Parks, State Office Building, Annapolis, MD 21404.

Massachusetts: Department of Natural Resources, 100 Cambridge Street, Boston, MA 02202, or Department of Commerce & Development, 150 Causeway Street, Boston, MA 02114.

Michigan: Division of Conservation, Stevens T. Mason Building, Lansing, MI 48926.

Minnesota: Vacation Information Center, Department of Business Development, St. Paul, MN 55101.

Mississippi: Travel Department, Agricultural & Industrial Board, 1504 State Office Building, Jackson, MS 39201.

Missouri: Division of Commerce & Industrial Development, 803 Jefferson Building, Jefferson City, MO 65101.

Montana: Recreations & Parks Division, Fish & Game Department, Helena, MT 59601.

Nebraska: Game, Forestation & Parks Commission, State Capitol, Lincoln, NE 68509.

Nevada: Department of Economic Development, Tourism-Travel Division, Carson City, NV 89701.

New Hampshire: Division of Economic Development, P.O. Box 856, Concord, NH 03301.

New Jersey: Department of Conservation & Economic Development 520 East State Street, Trenton, NJ 08609.

New Mexico: Department of Development, 113 Washington Avenue, Santa Fe, NM 87501.

New York: Travel Bureau, Department of Commerce, 112 State Street, Albany, NY 12207.

North Carolina: Travel & Promotion Division, Department of Conservation & Development, Raleigh, NC 27602.

North Dakota: Travel Department, State Capitol Building, Bismarck, ND 58501.

Ohio: Division of Parks & Recreation, Department of Natural Resources, 913 Ohio, Departments Building, Columbus, OH 43215.

Oklahoma: Industrial Development and Park Department, 500 Will Rogers Memorial Building, Oklahoma City, OK 73105.

Oregon: State Highway Division, Travel Information Section, 101 State Highway Building, Salem, OR 97310.

Pennsylvania: Department of Forests & Waters, Harrisburg, PA 17101.

Rhode Island: R.I. Development Council, Roger Williams Building, Hayes Street, Providence, RI 02908.

South Carolina: Department of Parks, Recreation & Tourism, P.O. Box 1358, Columbia, SC 29202.

South Dakota: Department of Highways, Travel Section, Pierre, SD 57501.

Tennessee: Division of State Parks, Tennessee Department of Conservation, 2611 West End Avenue, Nashville, TN 37203.

Texas: Travel & Information Division, Texas Highway Department, P.O. Box 5064, Austin, TX 78703.

Utah: Utah Travel Council, Council Hall, Capital Hill, Salt Lake City, UT 84114.

Vermont: Department of Forest & Parks, Montpelier, VT 05602.

Virginia: State Travel Service, Department of Conservation & Economic Development, 911 East Broad Street, Richmond, VA 23219.

Washington: State Parks & Recreation Commission, 522 S. Franklin, Olympia, WA 98501.

West Virginia: Department of Commerce, Travel Development Division, Room B-553, 1900 Washington Street, East Charleston, WV 25305.

Wisconsin: Conservation Department, Box 450, Madison, WI 53701.

Wyoming: Wyoming Travel Commission, 2320 Capitol Avenue, Cheyenne, WY 82001.

CANADA

Canadian Office of Travel
150 Kent Street
Ottawa, Canada K1A 0H6

Provincial Camping Information

Alberta: Alberta Department of Lands and Forests, Natural Resources Building, Edmonton 6, Alberta

British Columbia: British Columbia Department of Recreation and Conservation, Parliament Buildings, Victoria, British Columbia

Manitoba: Manitoba Department of Tourism, Recreation, and Cultural Affairs, Tourist Branch, 408 Norquay Building, Winnipeg, Manitoba

New Brunswick: New Brunswick Department of Natural Resources Tourism Development Branch, P.O. Box 1030, Fredericton, New Brunswick

Newfoundland: Parks Section, Resources Branch, Newfoundland Department of Mines, Agriculture, and Resources, St. John's, Newfoundland

Northwest Territories: Travel-Arctic, Government of the Northwest Territories, Yellowknife, Northwest Territories

188

Nova Scotia: Nova Scotia Department of Lands and Forests, P.O. Box 68, Truro, Nova Scotia

Ontario: Public Relations Branch, Ontario Ministry of Industry and Tourism, Queen's Park, Toronto, Ontario

Prince Edward Island: P.E.I. Department of Environment and Tourism, P.O. Box 2000, Charlottetown, Prince Edward Island

Quebec: Parks Branch, Department of Tourism, Fish, and Game, Parliament Buildings, Quebec City, Quebec

MEXICO

Mexican Government Department of Tourism offices are located at the following addresses:

United States

625 North Michigan Avenue
Ste. 1220
Chicago, Illinois, 60611

1800 Main St. Shop B
Ground Floor
Dallas, Texas, 75201

Cinderella City
701 West Hampden E. 2396
Inglewood, Colorado, 80110

Mellie Esperson Bldg.
805 Walker Avenue
Houston, Texas, 77002

3106 Wilshire Blvd.
Los Angeles, Calif. 90010

100 Biscayne
Tower Bldg., Suite 612
Miami, Florida, 33132

203 St. Charles St.
New Orleans, La. 70130

630 Fifth Avenue
New York, N.Y. 10020

3443 North Central Ave.
Financial Center, Suite 101
Phoenix, Arizona, 85012

400 N. St. Mary's St.
San Antonio, Texas, 78205

707 Broadway
The Home Tower, Suite 935
San Diego, California, 92101

219 Sutter St.
San Francisco, California, 94108

36 South Stone Avenue
Tuscon, Arizona, 85701

The Barr Bldg., Suite 104
914 17th St. N.W.
Washington, D.C. 20006

Canada

3 Place Ville Marie
Esso Bldg., Suite 20
Montreal 113, Quebec

Federal Bldg.
85 Richmond Street W.
Toronto 110, Ontario